SEW U

The *Built by Wendy* Guide to Making Your Own Wardrobe

SEW U

Wendy Mullin with Eviana Hartman

ILLUSTRATIONS BY BECI ORPIN

ADDITIONAL ILLUSTRATIONS BY AGNIESZKA GASPARSKA

BULFINCH PRESS | NEW YORK • BOSTON • LONDON

Bulfinch Press
Hachette Book Group
237 Park Avenue, New York, NY 10017
Visit our Web site at www.bulfinchpress.com

First Edition: September 2006
Fifth Printing, December 2008

Bulfinch is an imprint of Little, Brown and Company. The Bulfinch name and logo are trademarks of Hachette Book Group, Inc.

Library of Congress Cataloging-in-Publication Data

Mullin, Wendy.
  SEW U: The Built by Wendy guide to making your own wardrobe / Wendy Mullin with Eviana Hartman ; illustrations by Beci Orpin.—1st ed.
      p. cm.
  Includes index.
  ISBN: 978-0-8212-5740-1 (hardcover)
    1. Machine sewing. I. Hartman, Eviana. II. Title.

TT713.M85 2005
646.4'04—dc22   2005024947

Design by Goodesign

PRINTED IN CHINA

DEDICATED

To My Mom and My Grandma

CONTENTS

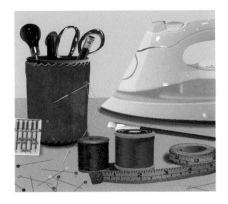

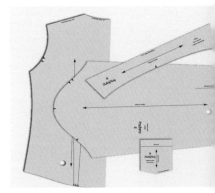

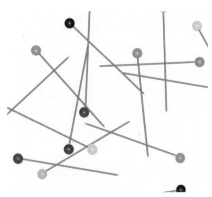

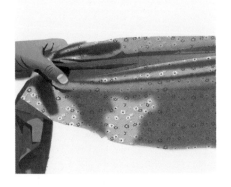

INTRODUCTION
COMMON THREADS

My Sewing Story, from Seamstress to Designer

TRUTH BE TOLD, I'VE ALWAYS HAD A LOVE/HATE RELATIONSHIP WITH SEWING.

Some of my earliest memories are of my mom dragging me to Vogue Fabrics in Evanston, Illinois, where I would sit for hours, bored out of my mind. She rewarded me for my patience by crafting matching outfits for me and my Barbies. This inspired me to sneak into her sewing room and steal expensive scraps of Ultrasuede to make my own doll clothing.

A few years later, in high school, I took a mandatory home ec class, where I learned the basics of sewing. My first project was a pink cotton jumper with a gathered drop waist—pretty unflattering, but easy enough to make, since there were no zippers or buttons to deal with. Suddenly, I got kind of excited about making clothes, and for the first time, I actually enjoyed going to the fabric store with my mom. She helped me pick out a pattern and printed fabric for a tent dress; I used the extra fabric to make a matching headband. From there, I grabbed some of my dad's old shirts and cut them apart, dyed them, and changed the buttons. I made skirts out of old jeans, painted my jackets, dyed my sweaters, and sewed appliqués onto anything and everything. When I graduated from high school, my grandpa matched the babysitting money I'd saved so I could buy my own sewing machine. It's the one I still use today.

In college, I taught myself more about patterns—the building blocks of any piece of clothing—by altering old ones I bought at garage sales for ten cents or cutting apart secondhand clothing and figuring out how it was constructed. I started sewing a few basic shapes, experimenting with the fabrics and trims to make them fresher, more flattering, cooler. Before I knew it, I was taking custom orders from dorm-mates and hemming pants for professors. With the extra cash I earned, I was even able to quit the graveyard shift at the doughnut shop. I went to classes during the day, sewed all night, and sent the pieces I made to a couple of local record stores in the Midwest to sell on consignment. (Why record stores? They were the only places I found inviting enough to shop in.)

After graduation, I moved to New York and spent a year at the Fashion Institute of Technology to pick up more technical skills. I did this while working at a record store in the East Village and slaving away at the sewing machine by night. I sold my clothes right there alongside the CDs and vinyl. On a whim, I made a few guitar straps for the musicians that shopped at the store. One thing led to another, and now, twelve years later, I have a thriving independent business, three stores, and a loyal following of creative, independent-minded customers—customers who, if they had the knowledge and tools, would be just as happy to make cool stuff for themselves. I named my company Built by Wendy as a twist on those old "Made by Grandma" labels—a nod to my home-sewing roots.

BOOK SMART
WHAT TO EXPECT

As a serious sewer, I've always been something of an anomaly among my friends. But things were different back in the day. If you were young and female, your mom taught you to sew, and you probably made at least some of your clothes. It was cheaper, it was personal, it was fulfilling. So what happened? For a while, sewing lost its cool. For one thing, the advent of feminism made the domestic arts, well, unfashionable. Why should women make their own clothes, the reasoning went, when they could be out working? Homemade clothes went the way of the home-cooked meal. Why spend hours laboring over a dress when you could buy something resembling what you wanted at a cheap-chic chain store? (Never mind if it was made of cheesy fabric and fell apart after a few nights out; it would probably be out of style by then anyway.)

If you're like me, the state of fashion today leaves you wanting more—a lot more. What ever happened to clothes made with love? (Haute couture doesn't count.) When I started my label, I wanted to emphasize quirky, homespun detail over obvious trends. And since then, I've seen some promising developments, especially in my downtown New York neighborhood. More and more creative, independent-minded, ultra-stylish people are dusting off mom's old machines or buying new ones, whether to follow their dreams of becoming designers or simply to express themselves. Sewing lets you make things that fit your body perfectly. It ensures that you won't look like a clone. You can customize the length, the color, the trim, the buttons, the thread, and all the other details on any garment to make it completely your own. And once you get the hang of the technical stuff, you'll be surprised by how fun and fulfilling—not to mention relaxing—the process is.

Because of what I do, quite a few of my friends have asked me to help them with their sewing projects. Their common complaints were that traditional sewing books were both daunting and dowdy, and that the sewing patterns available weren't consistent with current styling or fit. Chances are, you're not interested in mastering the art of making ruffled curtains or Christmas stockings (though if you are, the skills I teach you here will make it easier).

With this book, I'm not only offering sewing tips and tricks, but also the tools to create your own clothes. We'll focus on the essentials of a modern girl's wardrobe—the perfect A-line skirt, the shirt with a twist, and sexy pants—using the patterns that form the basis of my collection. I'll teach you how to customize everything from the fit to the pockets so that the designs are as much yours as mine. (And if you're too busy to sew them yourself, I'll also explain how to have a tailor realize your vision for you.) Sure, the tasks of pattern-making, cutting, and sewing can seem unglamorous—even I get bored and frustrated with them sometimes—but they're the foundation that allows your creativity to come to life.

If you've never attempted to make clothes before, the process probably seems a bit scary, and not just because you'll be operating a machine that seems capable of swiftly amputating your thumbs. Sewing is an industry unto itself, and there are so many different kinds of equipment, fabrics, trims, styles, techniques, and tricks that the mere act of entering a fabric store can be enough to send you fleeing in horror to the mall for your clothes. Besides, too many people, once they try to whip something up, end up with something resembling an asymmetrical potato sack (and not in a cool way). I'm here to change that.

This is not an exhaustive sewing manual. Instead, I've condensed the overwhelming amount of information out there so you can make some simple styles—styles you'll actually want to wear—relatively easily. Using my experience from twenty years of sewing and twelve years of designing my own label, I'll show you my favorite techniques for making clothes and how to get the most use out of three basic patterns.

Still scared? Don't be. Once you've measured yourself and cut out the three basic shapes that fit your body from my patterns, you'll be free to focus on the creative part of designing: choosing fabrics, flourishes, and trims. For each type of garment, I'll explain several ways to customize and rework the basic template, from changing the collar and sleeves on a shirt to adding ruffles or piping to a skirt. And once you've done this, you'll understand how clothes are constructed—which will enable you to rework your old clothes and revamp your entire wardrobe. Sure, the process can be tricky, and you're almost guaranteed to make a few mistakes along the way (I know I have!), but that's all part of the learning curve. If you stay organized, prepared, and patient, you'll find it's easier, and a lot more fun, than you think.

Finally, if you're brimming with ideas but just can't bring yourself to do the work, there's always Plan B: handing the blueprint for your vision over to your neighborhood tailor. I'll devote an entire chapter to this, from preparing your design to important talking points. But first, you'll gain a general understanding of how garments are put together—how they're *built,* if you will. Whether you're shooting to see your name on the racks at Saks or simply feeling crafty, it's knowledge that will never fail to come in handy.

OVERVIEW

HOW TO USE THIS BOOK (and how to get inspired)

Some people go through years of college just to learn how to make clothes. Others, like me, learn by trial and error over a period of decades. But whether you're a pro or you've never so much as glimpsed a sewing machine, this book has something for you.

Chapters 1 through 5 will help you set up your sewing room and supply kit, teach you about fabrics, notions, patterns, and cutting, and go over everything you need to know about sewing. If you're an experienced sewer, you might be able to skip these, but I think they're worth reading. I've crammed them full of my favorite improvised shortcuts and DIY organizing tips—the kind of secrets you won't find in stodgy sewing manuals.

Chapters 6, 7, and 8 are where we get down to business: making the clothes. Because this is the first book in what I hope will be a varied and useful series, I've chosen to focus here on the three basic elements that make up a core wardrobe for women: skirts, shirts, and pants. The three appear in order of difficulty.

I've included tissue-paper patterns—based on the ones I use in my collections—for each of the three types of garments. You can cut out the patterns in the size that fits you best (I'll explain how) to make perfect-fitting clothes. The main patterns are basic, but that doesn't mean that what you create has to be boring. Sure, everyone needs staples like black pants and white shirts, but I'll also show you several different varieties of skirts, shirts, and pants that you can create with slight pattern changes.

You can replicate my suggested projects from collar to hem, but you don't have to. From the starting point of the patterns, you can mix things up as much as you like—I'll give you some ideas in each of the project chapters.

Chapter 9 will explain how to work with a tailor if you find yourself short on time or prefer to have someone else sew your creations.

Beginner's Corner

If this is all new to you, proceed carefully. Yes, it's great to start dreaming up ideas, but before you try to make something, practice, practice, and practice some more.

The best way to begin is to set up a sewing room, stock it with supplies, and start reading. When you're out buying your sewing tools, grab some inexpensive fabric—now is not the time to blow a week's pay on Italian cashmere. I suggest picking up a twenty-five-yard bolt of cotton muslin, which is the low-cost fabric that even master couturiers use for trial runs before making the real thing.

Get to know the different functions of your sewing machine using muslin or another scrap fabric. As you read this book, try out the different techniques; once you understand how patterns work and you're comfortable with the act of sewing itself, you can throw yourself into the design process. But before you start your masterpiece, it's a good idea to cut out your pattern pieces and try making a test garment using muslin.

Recipe for Success: The Project Ticket

At the beginning of each project chapter (skirts, shirts, and pants), I've included what I call a project ticket. This is basically the "recipe" for your design—it organizes all the elements of any garment (fabrics, thread, trim, buttons, sketch, etc.) so you know what you have and what you need to fill in.

Make several photocopies of all three types of tickets and keep them on hand in your sewing area. Each time you start a new project, use a ticket as a guide. It may seem like an unnecessary extra step, but it will spell out your options clearly and serve as a reference point throughout the project. It's also an easy way to keep track of things that inspire you. Perhaps you've found a piece of shirting fabric you love. That is the starting point for a "recipe." Staple a swatch of the fabric in the appropriate place on a shirt ticket and design the rest around it. Look at the different "ingredients" you'll need to fill in and think about how you want them to look. Do you want to use contrast thread? Add piping? Make a lace collar instead of a classic pointed one?

Or perhaps you're feeling inspired by some oversize vintage buttons you found at a flea market. You decide to make pants, and tape one to the button section of the pant ticket. Now the next steps are right in front of you. What type of fabric would pair well with your buttons? What about pockets? And so it goes.

SKIRT PROJECT TICKET

STYLE: PREPPY SPRING SKIRT

TRIM NOTES:

* 7" navy zipper

PATTERN NOTES:

* shorten to mini length — no hem allowance needed to be included since we are covering the edge with bias binding
* use rounded patch pockets
* don't use facings
* cut contrast bias binding

SEWING NOTES:

* use bias binding around hem, pocket edges, and waist edge

FABRIC AND TRIMS:

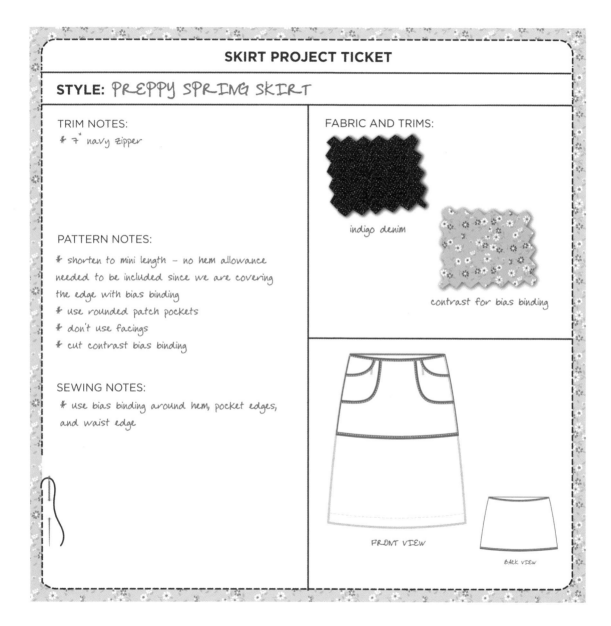

indigo denim

contrast for bias binding

FRONT VIEW

BACK VIEW

Getting Inspired

So you set up the perfect sewing space. You learn your way around your sewing machine, and patterns cease to remind you of a bad day in geometry class. Next comes the fun part: designing. I find inspiration for my collections in all sorts of places—foreign cultures, glamorous women throughout history, old movies—but believe it or not, the best source of creativity for any sewer is right in front of you: your closet.

Take a look at what you love and then figure out what's missing. Do you need lightweight linen trousers to pair with the peasant top you just picked up in Mexico? Do your brand-new fall boots cry out for a tweed skirt to show them off? Think about pieces you can incorporate into your wardrobe and think about what type of fabric and weight will suit them best. Go for colors and prints that match (or mis-match, if that's your preference) what you already have, because there's nothing worse than a painstak-ingly stitched new shirt logging quality time in your closet. After all, what's the point of sewing if you can't show off the fruits of your labor? (Or at least give them as gifts.)

Elements of Design

The patterns in this book can create simple staples if that's what you're after, but the possibilities are countless. You're the designer—you can do anything you want! There are several variables that can shake up the basic patterns:

Fabrics can completely alter the look, feel, and drape of a garment. Think about incorporating different prints, textures, weights, and colors.

Pattern details. Try playing with pockets, collars, sleeves, belt loops, ruffles, and types of seams.

Fit. You can change the fit before the garment is finished—this isn't nearly as hard as it sounds. You can lengthen a shirt hem, shorten a skirt, or widen or slim down the garment body.

Trims, such as buttons, pipings, zippers, appliqués, and lace, can make the difference between ordinary and extraordinary.

Thread colors and stitching. You might not have thought about this, but you can really add personality to a garment by using a totally unexpected thread color. Why not use punk neon pink stitching on a preppy blue oxford shirt? Or you might make a pair of dark denim pants extraspecial by topstitching them with shimmering gold.

In my experience, the idea that sparks a new design is often only one piece of the puzzle. The element that inspires you will set some limitations, and from there you can make design decisions. Say you find a swatch of lightweight cotton fabric in a pale blue floral print. You certainly can't make pants. But you can make a skirt or a shirt. Do you *need* a flower-print skirt? Or a top to go with it? Will this color be flattering on your lower body? Will it flatter your coloring if you make a shirt? Would a shirt be easier to wear year-round?

Perhaps you've decided the blue sets off your eye color but wouldn't slim your lower body. A shirt it is. Now you have more things to consider. Which shape do you like—a streamlined, boyish oxford or something girlier? What about buttons—would decorative white ones look good? Would small, subtle ones look better? Perhaps big ones would be too much with the print. What about thread? Would contrast topstitching look too heavy? Do you need or want pockets? Do you want short sleeves or long sleeves? A round or pointed collar? Consider every aspect of the design, and you'll be surprised by how creative you can get.

Collage Education: How to Create an Idea Book or Board

Ideas can come from the unlikeliest of places; for one collection, I mixed English country prep school influences with an eighties Rebecca De Mornay-in-*Risky Business* vibe. Cobbling together a scrapbook or corkboard of images and objects that inspire me helps paint a fuller picture of what I want to make in the longer run. (I'm not alone; pretty much every designer does this.) First, there's the obvious: Read fashion magazines and tear out pages you like for inspiration. But don't limit yourself to copying what you see on the runways. Hit used bookstores for undiscovered gems about fashion, art, and film. Look through your mother's—and grandmother's—photo albums. Visit museums, pick up trinkets and fabrics at thrift shops and flea markets, and snap plenty of pictures when you travel. Combine all these with your favorite fabric swatches, trims, and buttons, and before you know it, the ideas will start flowing.

Bonus Round: Customizing

Maybe there are some pieces that you never wear but can't bear to part with. These have the potential to become something else. Perhaps you love the fabric but hate the fit, or are bored with a basic but don't want to toss it out. Well, there are a million things you can do to make an old garment new again: You can make shorts or skirts out of pants, change buttons, add trim, change sleeve lengths on a shirt, add a ruffle to just about anything, dye something, or even combine two garments to make one amazing new thing. Think creatively!

Finally, take a closer look at the pieces you know you'll never wear. What can you salvage that would make great trim? You might want to remove buttons to sew onto something else, save lace to reattach as ruffles, or even cut silk screens out of T-shirts to use as patches. When in doubt, hang on to what you've got—you never know when inspiration will strike.

EXTREME MAKEOVERS: SOME IDEAS FOR RESURRECTING OLD CLOTHES

Older brother's rock T-shirt:
Why save this treasure for sleeping? Slim it down easily by sewing along the dotted lines.

Baggy khaki pants:
Reinvent a frumpy pair of pants by turning them into shorts. Hem the legs, roll them up, and use the leftover fabric to make side tabs. Swap the old buttons for cute decorative ones.

Dated overalls:
Don't toss those tie-dyed overalls from your secret past as a hippie. Dye them dark navy or black, and turn the legs into a short skirt. This looks unexpectedly polished over a ribbed tank top or white oxford shirt.

BEFORE AFTER

——— CUT LINE
- - - - - SEWING LINE

BEFORE

AFTER

BEFORE

AFTER

CHAPTER 1
GETTING IN GEAR

Setting Up Your Tool Kit and Sewing Room

If I had to, I could get by with some craft scissors, a few soup cans, a needle, and a pencil. I'm not suggesting you do the same, but it *is* worth knowing that you don't need to shell out a month's rent on newfangled gadgets at the fabric store just to stitch up a shirt. Because I'm mostly self-taught—and because I started my career as a broke college student—I've found ways to sew with barely any supplies over the years. Still, there are a few things any beginner ought to have, so I've made a list of the basics. Once you get more advanced and have a better sense of what you like and don't like to work with, you might want to invest in some fancier stuff. I'll include some of it here.

TOOLS
IT'S OKAY TO BREAK THE RULES

As a foundation for any sewer, these are the things a well-stocked tool kit should have.

1. SCISSORS AND CUTTERS

When I first started sewing, I did my cutting with orange-handled craft scissors—you know, the same kind you probably have sitting in your junk drawer. (But good luck trying to sew with those—once they've cut paper, they won't cut fabric. Trust me.) I used the orange scissors because I had no idea there was anything else out there. One day, in the fabric store, I saw the woman behind the counter sharpening a fierce-looking pair of eight-inch shears from a company called Gingher. They were thirty dollars, which was a lot of money at the time—in fact, it still sounds like a huge price to pay for scissors. But she convinced me that they were a must-have and promised that if I took care of them I'd have them for several decades. I bought them, and I still use the same pair.

You can get by with shears alone—I suggest the eight-inch size—but you might want to have some other types of scissors on hand as well:

Regular Scissors. If you find yourself cutting paper for your project (for instance, to reinforce your tissue patterns for long-term use), then you must use regular scissors.

Pinking Shears have a zigzag edge, which some sewers like to use for finishing seams and decorative edges.

Rotary Cutter and Mat. Some people prefer this system for cutting fabrics and patterns; it's faster, more precise, easier to use with slippery fabrics, and gentler on your wrists. (Plus, there's something kind of fun about using a rotary cutter; it's like a superfast pizza cutter.) When I first started selling clothes in college, I didn't have a seamstress or factory—I made everything myself. I'd make three dresses at a time, conveyor-belt style, and I'd cut several layers of fabric together—that is, until my right wrist hurt so much I could barely take notes in class. Eventually, I gave in and got a rotary cutter, and it made my life easier.

If you buy a cutter, do *not* try to use it without a mat (unless, for some reason, you actually *want* your table to have lines carved all over the surface.) And never use a rotary cutter to cut notches on your pattern; it's great for big, long slices, but it's not the most delicate instrument. You could easily cut right into the body of the garment (ouch!), so use shears for notches instead.

Small Embroidery Scissors. I prefer these for little cuts, like trimming seams and clipping threads, but they're totally optional. Mine have a pretty golden-stork design. I tied a ribbon through them so I can wear them around my neck for easy access during sewing.

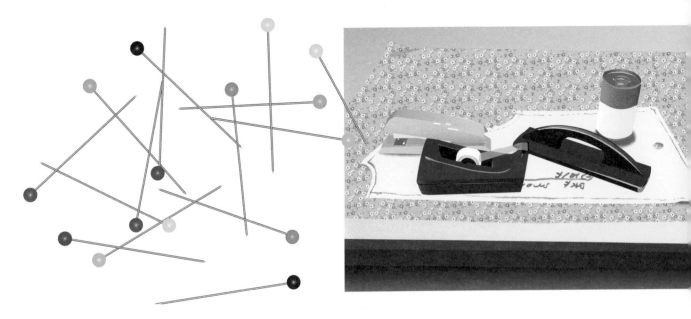

2. PINS AND WEIGHTS

When you think of sewing, a pincushion stuck with pins is probably one of the first things to come to mind, right? But, believe it or not, there have been times when I haven't had pins. Straight pins are the standard tool for securing your pattern to the fabric for the cutting process and pinning your garment together in preparation to sew. But when times were tight, I came up with alternatives. You can staple your garment pieces along the seam allowance edge (outside the seam line) or hand-sew a couple of little stitches on a few points along the seam to hold it together. You can use weights to secure the pattern to the fabric when you're cutting, which works especially well if you're using a rotary cutter. Weights are a faster option than pinning around each pattern and are available at most sewing stores. You can also improvise and use some soup cans or any small, heavy object such as a stapler or tape dispenser. Or pick up some metal washers at the hardware store.

Straight pins vary in size and length. The most common variety are #17 dressmaker pins. I like glass-head pins because they are colorful, and the little ball on the end is easy to handle. Plus, they're easy to see when you drop them on the floor. (I used to sew in my bedroom at my parents' house, cutting fabric on the carpeted floor. It was a nightmare trying to find flat-head silver pins stuck in the carpet, and I stepped on them—sharp end up—more than once. Believe me, it's not a feeling you want to experience for yourself!)

TIP

Need to pick up scattered pins from your floor? Tape a magnet from your fridge onto a broom handle and slowly run the magnetic wand over the floor.

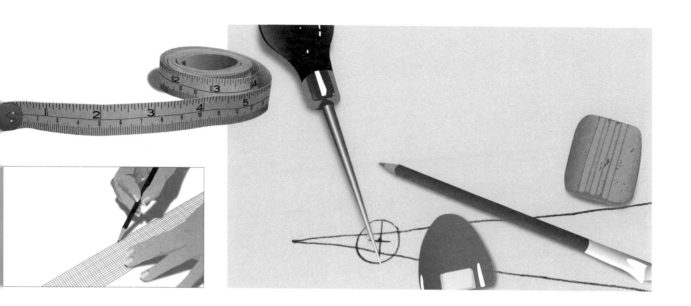

3. TAPE MEASURE

This is the classic yellow sixty-inch cloth tape. In a pinch, you can also use a belt to take measurements, and then lay the belt alongside a ruler to determine the measurements in inches.

4. CLEAR PLASTIC RULER

An 18″ by 2″ ruler is an invaluable tool for taking flat measurements on patterns and drafting custom pattern pieces.

5. MARKING TOOLS

In general, as long as you mark lightly and within the area that will be covered by sewing, you can use a regular pencil. But remember to be especially careful on light-colored, lightweight fabric, since you might see the marks through the fabric.

#2 Pencil. As long as you mark lightly, this works great for marking dart points or pocket placements.

Tailor's Chalk or Wax. Chalk can be brushed off after marking; wax melts off when you iron it. Both are good options for dark fabrics, on which light pencil marks might not be visible.

Water-Soluble Markers are supposed to rub off with a dab of water, but in my experience the mark doesn't always come out.

Disappearing-Ink Markers, which you can find at fabric stores, are a safer bet, unless your sewing project will take place over a long period of time, as the ink vanishes after a couple of days.

Awl. This pointed object, which you can find in any hardware store or handy person's tool kit, can be used to punch holes to mark dart points. It's easy and fast, but be careful not to damage the fabric. I don't recommend using one when working with delicate fabrics.

Spiked Wheel and Colored Wax Paper. This is another marking system that produces dotted lines on fabric quickly and precisely. It's good, for instance, for marking the shape of a dart if it's not straight.

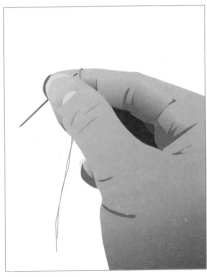

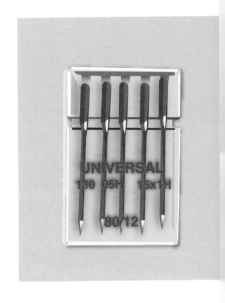

6. SEAM RIPPER

This inexpensive, invaluable tool can be found in any chain drugstore, and I highly recommend getting one—in fact, get two or three so you'll always have one on hand in case one disappears (they're tiny). It's the most precise way to correct sewing mistakes by opening seams, and it's also useful if you're going to be altering clothes you already have. If you use your shears instead, you'll probably end up ripping the fabric or stretching out the seam. Not worth it! It's better to cut each stitch instead of ripping down the center of the seam and tearing. It's more time-consuming, but it's safer than potentially ruining your whole project.

7. HAND-SEWING NEEDLES

Sewing machines are great and all, but there are some delicate tasks, like sewing on buttons and certain types of trim, that can only be done by hand. Sharps are the basic type of needle you'll need for most sewing projects involving woven fabrics (nonknits). They come in sizes 1 through 10; size 1 is the heaviest (used for denims) and size 10 is the lightest (used for delicate fabrics like silks). My advice? Buy a multipack that has a variety of sizes. For cotton shirts, I use a size 8. For sewing a button onto twill pants, I use a 3. If you'll be working with knit fabrics, use ballpoint needles instead.

8. MACHINE NEEDLES

These come in sizes 7 through 18, but the numbers work the opposite way from those of hand-sewing needles: machine needles with higher numbers are for heavier fabrics and the lower numbers are for lightweight, delicate fabrics. The most common all-purpose needle is a universal point, and again, I suggest buying a multisize pack. However, machine needles can break, so make sure you have backup needles for your fabric type to cover yourself in case of a mishap (especially if you're a novice). For most basic shirting fabrics, you'll use a size 10 to 12. There are also special-size needles for knits (which are again ballpoint needles), denims, and leather. Be sure you're using the appropriate one for your fabric!

  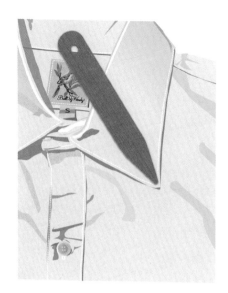

9. THREAD

Thread comes in a dizzying array of thicknesses and materials. You'll find cotton, polyester, silk, and all sorts of combinations. For the projects in this book, you can use an all-purpose mercerized cotton–wrapped polyester thread. As a general rule of thumb, use heavier thread for heavier fabrics and lighter thread for more delicate fabrics. When matching thread color to fabric, always go a shade darker if you need to make a choice. Sometimes you might want to use a completely different shade of thread for contrast—I've made navy pants with white thread, for instance.

10. IRON

A clean steam iron is essential to any sewing project. You'll use it to prepare your fabric and press open seams during the sewing process. I suggest getting the best one you can afford; your miniature travel iron isn't going to cut it.

11. IRONING BOARD

This makes ironing easier and creates another work area—and the more surfaces you have to work with, the better. Make sure the cover is clean or you'll end up pressing old stains onto your new shirt. Before I had an ironing board, I would spread towels on my floor and use them as an ironing surface.

12. PRESSING CLOTH

The last thing you want is an iron-shaped burn mark on the backside of your brand-new pants. A pressing cloth goes between your garment and the iron to prevent heat damage. If you don't want to buy one, you can substitute an old T-shirt or another scrap of fabric.

13. WOODEN POINT

This tool is used to dry-press small, hard-to-reach areas during the sewing process. You can run the wooden point over a seam to temporarily press it open. It's also used to push points of collar tips to the maximum—it's a much better option than sticking a sharp object in there. I tried using a pen once and ended up ripping right through the collar!

Logo Mania:
A Few Reliable Brands

Buying something just because of the label is not my philosophy when it comes to fashion. Still, when it's time to invest in a sewing machine, it helps to know who the major players are. Plus, buying a major brand means you'll find more places to service your machine. This list is by no means exhaustive, but it's worth keeping in mind:

* BERNINA
* SINGER
* BROTHER
* PFAFF
* SIMPLICITY

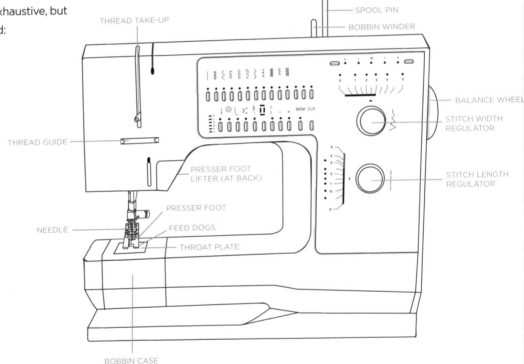

THREAD TAKE-UP

SPOOL PIN

BOBBIN WINDER

THREAD GUIDE

PRESSER FOOT LIFTER (AT BACK)

BALANCE WHEEL

STITCH WIDTH REGULATOR

STITCH LENGTH REGULATOR

PRESSER FOOT

NEEDLE

FEED DOGS

THROAT PLATE

BOBBIN CASE

READY, SET, INVEST
HOW TO SHOP FOR A SEWING MACHINE

When I first started sewing, I used my mom's twenty-year-old Bernina—until, as mentioned before, my grandpa helped me buy my own. I've been using the same machine—a Bernina 1090—since my high school graduation, and I couldn't be happier with it (in spite of its silly new wave–style paintbrush-stroke design). I've grown accustomed to its features and feel. Think of your machine as an investment: If you take care of it by cleaning and oiling it regularly, it will last forever, and your projects will run smoothly.

That said, how much to spend—and what features to look for—depends on just how much sewing you plan on doing. Some of the features on top-of-the-line models—computerized buttonholes, elaborate embroidery at the touch of a button—aren't really worth the money, in my opinion. The projects in this book are fairly simple and should be doable with just about any machine—even mom's old one! Still, you should count on spending at least a hundred dollars if you're buying a new machine. Those twenty-dollar minimachines are probably fine for hemming the occasional pair of pants, but if yours breaks midproject, you might end up throwing it out the window in a fit of rage—and who knows how much a new window costs? More than a good machine, I suspect.

When in doubt, visit a dealer with floor models and try them out to see which one feels right. Ask lots of questions. In general, you should look for a machine that's constructed solidly (if it wobbles, that's a bad sign). Since I have always sewn on my Bernina, I take what it can do for granted. I once bought a cheap machine to use at home and realized that it was slow, its bobbin was difficult to wind, and its feet were a pain to change. It makes more sense to invest in a better machine because it makes the whole experience much more pleasurable, your projects will come out better, and the machine will last longer. The features you'll require will depend on what you'll be doing, but here are the ones that save me a lot of time and effort:

MACHINE SHELL
A metal shell usually means a machine will last longer and feel more sturdy. Plastic just seems kind of cheap to me, but then again, it's lighter and easier to move around if that's a concern.

AUTOMATIC BOBBIN WINDER
Bobbins (the spools that hold the bottom thread in a stitch) aren't very big, and you'll be tearing through them at an alarming rate. A machine that winds them quickly and easily will be your friend. Also, look for a machine whose bobbin pops out easily—you don't want to have to unscrew twenty small pieces just to reach your bobbin.

AUTOMATIC BUTTONHOLE FEATURE
Take a look at a buttonhole on your shirt—does that look like something you'd want to snip and stitch yourself? Didn't think so. Luckily, most new machines come with this lifesaving feature, even less-expensive ones.

REMOVABLE PRESSER FEET
The presser foot holds the fabric down during sewing. However, in certain cases (like when you'll be sewing on a zipper), you'll need to change the presser foot midproject. How easily can this be done? It's something to keep in mind while shopping. On some machines, you have to unscrew the feet, which is annoying. I prefer the type that requires only a simple flip of a lever.

ZIGZAG STITCH
Not all stitches should be straight, especially if you're working with stretch fabrics. If your machine provides options, all the better.

SPEED
Sewing is a long process anyway, so you definitely don't want the machine to hold you back.

SPACE ODYSSEY
CREATING A COMFORTABLE PLACE TO SEW

Before you sew one stitch, it's important to set up a clean, organized space for your projects, where all your supplies are easily accessible. Here's how:

Hit the Spot

Set aside an area or room that is either solely for sewing or can be easily converted into a sewing area. I know this is easier said than done—after all, I am a New Yorker. In my first Manhattan apartment, I used to keep my supplies under my bunk bed (which I shared with a roommate) and cut my fabric on the floor. I didn't have enough electrical outlets, so I always had to unplug my machine to iron. But at least I kept everything organized and together in one storage tub!

Let There Be Light

Sewing is all about focusing on small details. If you can't see them, you might mess up—or, worse, poke yourself with a needle. It's important to have good lighting in your sewing area. A space near a window, flooded with natural light, is ideal; I also recommend getting a powerful lamp.

Turning the Tables: Ideal Sewing Surfaces

SEWING TABLE

For your machine, look for a table that's on the lower side so you can sit up straight and still maneuver around. During the sewing process, you'll be hunched over quite a bit, so make sure to straighten and stretch often.

CUTTING TABLE

Laying out large swaths of fabric requires plenty of space. Most of us simply use the floor or the dining-room table. Another option is to get a sheet of plywood and cover it with kraft paper, which is easily discarded and replaced. Place the plywood on top of a table to create a large, clean work surface that you don't have to worry about scratching.

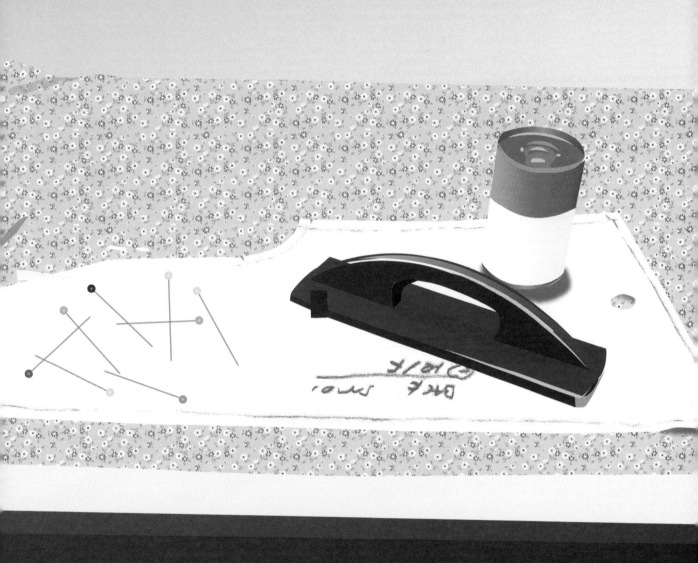

SECRET WEAPON:
THE CANVAS TOOL BAG

When in doubt—or when you're stuck with a closet-size dorm room or studio—keep everything in a tool bag with an open top and plenty of pockets around the sides to hold your supplies. It's a good size for storing everything, and it can easily be stowed away.

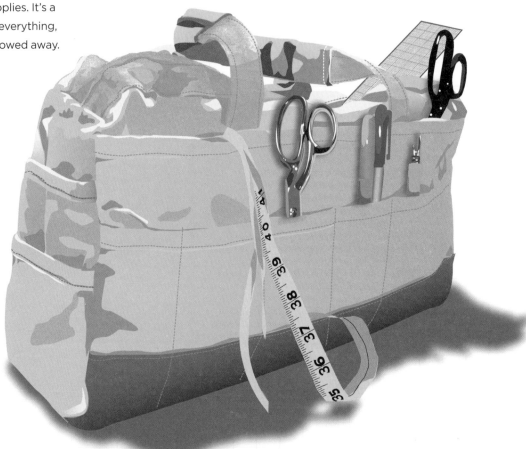

GET ORGANIZED

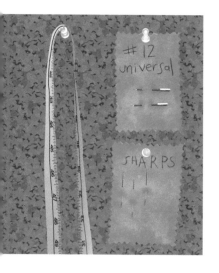

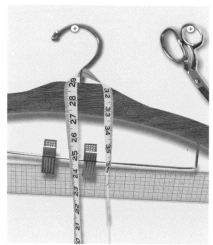

NEEDLES

Once hand and machine needles are out of their original packaging, it's almost impossible to tell them apart. Some of my favorite tricks for keeping track:

* Divide a corkboard into sections that denote sizes and types of needles, perhaps by covering different areas with different colors of fabric.

* Mark needle tips with colored nail polish to indicate each size and type.

* Use a marker to label each slice of a tomato-shaped pincushion and put needles in their corresponding sections.

THREAD

Hammer nails in rows on a piece of wood to make a thread holder and hang it on the wall to keep it out of your way. This device is also good for holding extra bobbins. To keep thread from unwinding or getting tangled, wrap a Post-it note around the cylinder. This will also protect the thread from dust and dirt.

SCISSORS, TAPE MEASURES, AND RULERS

It's better to have these things within easy reach than buried in a drawer or bin. Hang scissors and tape measures from hooks on the wall; for rulers, attach a clip to the wall and clip them on.

PENS, PENCILS, AWL, SEAM RIPPER, AND PINS

Store your marking tools and seam ripper in a tin can; cover the can with felt and stick your pins on the outside.

PINS, PART TWO

Apply magnetic spray or tape to the wall and stick your pins there. This will be especially convenient on a wall near your cutting and sewing surfaces.

CHAPTER 2
LIVING IN A MATERIAL WORLD

Fabrics, Notions, and Trims

Frankly, fabric stores used to freak me out. If you've never been in one before, you might feel the same way on your first visit. *Wait, why are there ten different kinds of white cotton? Why do some of them cost ten times as much as others? What if one of those tree-size bolts of fabric falls on my head?*

But you don't need to be intimidated; you just need to understand what it is you're looking for, and the process will become fun, not frustrating. (It's the same principle that applies to shopping in bookstores and record stores.) The fabric you choose for a project is the most important part of the look you'll end up with. So let's start with an existential question: Just what *is* fabric, anyway?

WOVEN FABRIC

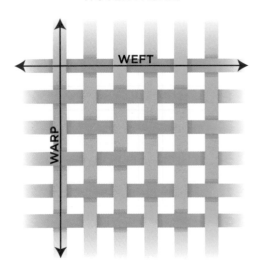

KNIT FABRIC

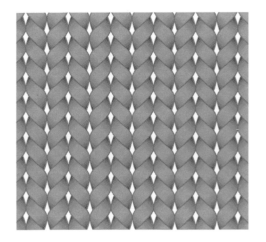

FABRIC TYPES

PLAIN

TWILL

SATIN

Fabrics start as fibers, which come either from nature (cotton, silk, linen) or from a laboratory (polyester and its many cousins). These fibers are spun into yarns, which are then woven or knitted into fabric.

Woven fabrics have vertical (warp) yarns and horizontal (weft) yarns, crisscrossed together to form a solid sheet of fabric. Some different types of weaves are plain weave (the strongest weave), twill weave (which features a diagonal design), and satin weave (which looks like it sounds—it has a smooth face).

Knit fabrics are made from interlocking loops of yarn. Generally speaking, knits tend to stretch. T-shirts are made of knits; so are socks. Some types of knits are jerseys (this refers to a type of knit, but many soft, stretchy knits fall into this category), rib knits (think of your favorite old Hanes tank), and interlocks (which are usually thicker than jerseys).

This book focuses mostly on woven fabrics. Why? Knits have enough unique properties (different methods for sewing and cutting, supplies needed, fit issues) to warrant a book of their own. (Don't be surprised if I come out with one.) The projects in this book can be made with knits, but be aware that you'll need to use a special needle and a zigzag stitch, and you'll need to reinforce some seams with stiffening tape.

I like to work with natural fabrics— they're more breathable and they suit my aesthetic. But you can sew with anything that feels good, looks good, and has the right weight for what you're going to be making. (More about that last point in a minute.)

BUYING FABRICS

It can be easy to spend three hours in a fabric store, adrift like a lost sailor. It can also be easy to get in and out quickly—that is, if you figure out in advance what you want to make and what you want to work with. If you'll be making summer pants, for instance, it's best to avoid the heavy-wool area; if you're making a dressy shirt, don't bother browsing the polar fleece section. (Then again, if you do have some time to spare, browse away—you might get inspired to do something totally new and different.) I could devote the length of the *Oxford English Dictionary* to describing every type of fabric out there, but for the sake of simplicity, I'll stick to recommendations based on the styles in this book.

Shirt Fabrics

When I first started sewing, I always got excited and overwhelmed by the shirting section of the fabric store—so many colors, prints, stripes, and textures to choose from! The classic button-front shirt will never go out of style, so you can always count on fabric stores to stock lots of ginghams and pinstripes. These are good fabrics to learn to sew with because they are easy to handle, cheap, always in stock, and because the stripes (which on gingham are both vertical and horizontal) make it easy to stay on grain and sew straight. (We'll learn about that later, but for now you'll just have to take my word for it.)

COTTON

Personally, I love using this for shirts because it's sturdy, breathable, and washable. It's easy to sew and handle, unlike silk, which can be very slippery. The only downside is its serious shrinkability—you should wash and dry cotton fabric three times before you cut it. Cotton for shirts comes in a variety of prints (floral, novelty, graphic), plaids, stripes, and solids. Some basic types of cotton fabric include the following:

Voile. A slightly sheer, summer-weight cotton.

Batiste. A medium-weight plain-weave fabric.

Lawn and poplin. Popular, crisp plain-weave cottons.

Oxford has a very smooth finish and a slight sheen—this is the classic men's dress shirt fabric.

Chambray. This rustic fabric, usually pale blue, looks a bit like denim but is lighter and more breathable.

Flannel is soft and fuzzy—just be sure you pay attention to the direction of the nap (the fuzzy part) when you cut! (See chapter 4 for more about that.)

SILK AND SYNTHETIC SUBSTITUTES

If you want a dressier, nighttime look, silk is the way to go. Real silk is much smoother and more elegant than the polyester versions, but, alas, it's more expensive.

Charmeuse is super shiny on one side and very slippery.

Chiffon is beautifully sheer. Just don't err on the small side when you choose a size, because chiffon looks better when it has room to billow and drape.

Washed silk has a cool, distressed look—and you can actually wash it!

Skirt Fabrics

It all depends on the season. For warmer months, shirt fabrics, like lightweight cottons, are great for skirts, but keep in mind that these tend to be sheer. (A pair of flesh-toned boy shorts can easily remedy the situation.) For maximum mileage, I recommend midweight fabrics like twill and thick washed silk—they'll work with summer tanks *and* fall sweaters. Heavier fabrics like tweed and wool look great with tights and boots in winter—you will, however, need to buy lining fabric (inexpensive synthetic satin that prevents unsightly cling). My personal favorites for skirts are cotton and wool, but you can also use silks and even cotton knits, like sweatshirt fabric.

COTTON

Available in a myriad of colors and weights, cotton is good for casual and sporty looks.

Denim. Who doesn't love a denim skirt? You might try lighter-weight or stretch denim to make sitting down more comfortable—stiff denim skirts, I've found, have an unfortunate tendency to shimmy upward and rotate around as you walk. Be sure to use the appropriate needle and thread.

Twill is a type of cotton with a diagonal weave. It's generally heavier and stiffer than shirting cottons, and therefore good for lower-body garments.

Canvas is a tightly woven fabric that is strong and durable.

Lightweight cottons used for shirts can also be used for skirts. If they are very sheer, though, you might want to double the layers.

WOOL

Available in a variety of weights and finishes, wool will keep you warm. Using wool for skirts generally requires a lining.

Gabardine is tightly woven. It is used for men's suits for a very polished look. Thicker wools, like camel hair, pair nicely with chunky sweaters for that elusive Ali MacGraw–in–*Love Story* look.

Tweed is a textured, flecked fabric that's an autumn classic and great for skirts.

Bouclé is similar to tweed but with a curly, looped finish—note that thicker versions might add undesired bulk to skirts.

Herringbones are twill weaves using two colors of yarn, creating a zigzag effect.

SILKS

These drape around the contours of your lower body, so an A-line skirt in silk will hang very differently than the same skirt in stiff denim or tweed. This is worth keeping in mind if one of your goals is to disguise figure flaws.

Pant Fabrics

For slim-fitting pants, it's important to use heavier fabric. The fabric weight should be marked on the bolt; for pants, shoot for something in the nine-to-twelve-ounce range. For heavier fabrics, like twelve-to-fourteen-ounce denims, you'll need a heavier sewing machine and needles. Also, be wary of buying complicated prints or horizontal stripes, which might not be too flattering on your lower half. When it comes down to it, you can, technically speaking, make pants out of any material. But realistically, there are a few things to remember. Pants get a lot of wear, and the seams are stretched every which way when you walk or sit down. For that reason, sheer, delicate fabrics like silk chiffon or cotton voile are basically off-limits.

COTTON AND COTTON BLENDS

For durability, it's not a bad idea to choose cotton with a small amount of polyester in the blend to help ward off wrinkles and stains.

Denim. Needless to say, denim goes with everything. A trouser pattern sewn in denim provides a great compromise between dressed-up and dressed-down. Generally, when you buy denim, it's been heavily treated, so it's very dark and stiff. Make sure to wash the fabric before you sew because it will soften and lighten a great deal when washed. (Unless you're one of those people who simply can't bear to wash their dark, stiff jeans—ever. I know the type.) In any case, stick with nine-to-twelve-ounce denim. Anything lighter is not durable enough for pants, and anything heavier might tax your sewing machine.

Corduroy. Okay, I won't insult your intelligence—you know what this is. It's warm, flattering, and one of my all-time favorites for casual fall and winter pants. It's available in thin to wide wales (the thickness of the vertical lines)—the wale number on the fabric tag will refer to the number of vertical lines in an inch of fabric. Stay away from lightweight 21-wale for pants—it's too light (but it does make a great shirt).

Moleskin is a soft, napped, durable cotton. The fuzzy finish makes it warm and comfortable—just remember that napped fabrics are one-way fabrics, and cut carefully! Moleskin is also known for attracting lint, so keep a roller on hand.

Twill is more durable and less stain prone than plain-weave cotton—two reasons I recommend it for summer pants over something lighter and more see-through.

WOOL

Try making pants out of men's suiting fabrics such as wool gabardine and pinstriped wool. They're polished and chic enough for formal offices and big nights out, yet they also look kind of cool contrasted against an old T-shirt or sweatshirt. Watch out for itchy wools, though. Try to stick to lighter-weight tropical wools or even wool-Lycra blends.

TIP

Feel free to mix fabrics for the small detail pieces in your garment. Try making the inside fly of your jeans out of floral shirting fabric or the pocket flap of your corduroy shirt out of denim.

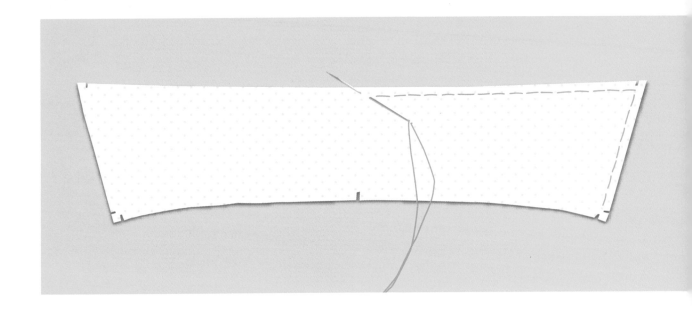

Back Story: All About Interfacings

Sometimes, fabric needs a little bit of extra help. Interfacing is a special kind of supportive fabric that's attached to the back of your fabric and is invisible when the finished garment is worn. It adds reinforcement and shape to collars, buttonholes, shoulder seams, and necklines.

Fusible interfacing can be ironed onto the back of your fabric so you don't have to bother sewing it on. This is a great option for most durable, traditional fabrics.

Don't skimp on price when buying fusible interfacing, though—cheap fusibles have poor-quality adhesives that don't iron on smoothly and will tear easily.

Stitchable (traditional) interfacing is a safer bet for:

* Synthetic and napped fabrics (corduroy and velvet), which might melt with the heat of the iron.

* Delicate silks, which are also heat-sensitive.

* Stain- and water-resistant fabrics, which repel the heat-bonding chemicals. When in doubt, ask your fabric dealer.

Interfacing isn't a one-size-fits-all support system. It comes in a plethora of different colors and weights; choose one that won't show through your fabric and has about the same thickness and drape. Ask for help if you're having trouble deciding.

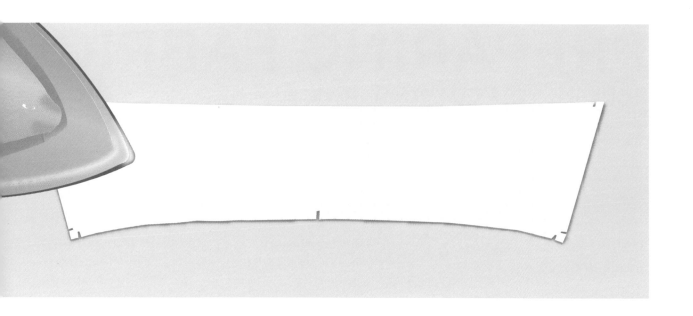

Stretching the Truth: A Note about Fabrics That Give a Little Bit

These days, thanks to the wonders of technology, plenty of rigid fabrics like cotton and wool have 1 to 5 percent synthetic stretch fibers woven in—but they don't look like typical stretchy fabrics. This type of fabric gives you the best of both worlds—comfort and flexibility with the polish of a traditional woven fabric—so don't be afraid to try it out. However, if you're making pants out of stretch fabric, you might want to go a size down (especially if you're between sizes anyway) so they fit snugly. Loose, stretched-out stretch pants don't look so hot.

How Much Fabric Should I Buy?

Fabrics are sold by the yard, but they come in different widths. Most shirting comes in 44"-wide bolts, and "bottom-weight" fabric—heavier, pants-appropriate stuff—tends to come in widths of 58". The greater the width, the more pattern pieces you can fit on the layout and the less yardage you'll need to buy. However, with one-way fabrics, all the pattern pieces need to be cut in the same direction, so you will need to buy extra fabric. See the chart below for my three basic patterns and the estimated yardage you'll need for each garment. It's always better to buy more fabric than less—you can always make a bag, pencil case, or scarf with the leftovers.

FABRIC WIDTH	SKIRT	SHIRT	PANT
44"–45"	1⅝ yds.	2 yds.	2½ yds.
58"–60"	1 yd.	1½ yds	2⅝ yds.

PREPARING FABRIC
BEFORE YOU CUT AND SEW

The Incredible Shrinking Fabric

Wash and dry your fabric according to its general care instructions—you should probably do this several times if you're using cotton, the most shrinkable of fabrics (ask your fabric-store salesperson for advice). Why bother preshrinking? It should be obvious—there's nothing worse than spending hours creating a masterpiece only to have it become too small the first time you wash it. Think ahead.

Ironing Out the Kinks

Once you've washed and dried the fabric, it's time to meet the press. Don't go a step further before you break out the iron: Crinkled fabric will throw off your pattern measurements during cutting and it's difficult to sew. When pressing, iron in the lengthwise direction of the fabric grain—in other words, parallel to the selvage (the finished edge) of the fabric. This will prevent it from stretching out, because the lengthwise grain is the strongest. (More about that in a minute.)

Getting to Know Your Fabric

Most fabrics, aside from knits (which have looped fibers, another category entirely), are woven in two directions. The lines of the weave have to be determined precisely before you place the pattern pieces on the fabric. And, in case they've shifted, they have to be pulled (in sewing lingo, blocked) into place so that they meet at an exact 90-degree angle. Otherwise, your clothes will look—and hang—off-kilter. The catch? You can't always see exactly where these lines are, and when you're handling a huge swath of fabric, eyeballing it won't work. Here's what you need to know (the term grainline refers to the direction of the weave):

Lengthwise grain (a.k.a. warp). This is the up-and-down direction of the fabric, and it is the strongest part of the weave. This grainline runs parallel to the selvage edge.

Crosswise grain (a.k.a. weft). This runs from selvage to selvage (horizontally, if you prefer to think of it that way) and has more give.

TIPS

No. 1: Before you wash, sew a basting stitch along each raw edge to prevent the fabric from fraying too much.

No. 2: If you're working with a dry-clean-only fabric, as annoying as it sounds, you should dry-clean it first.

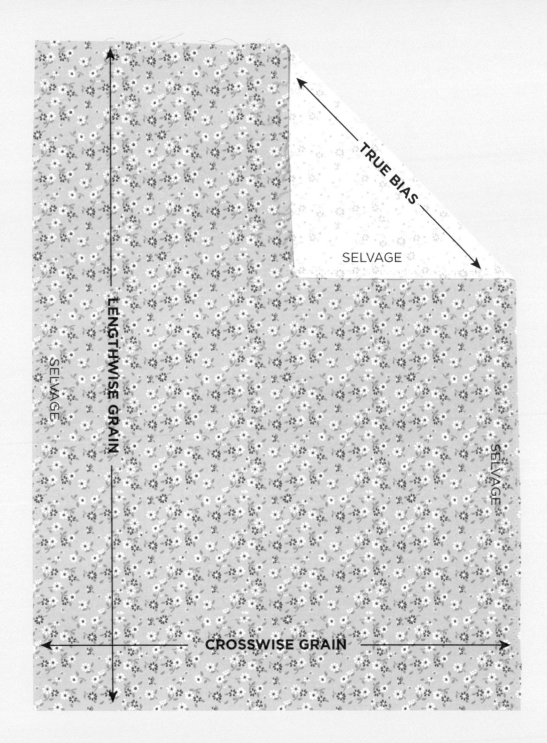

TRUE BIAS

SELVAGE

LENGTHWISE GRAIN

SELVAGE

SELVAGE

CROSSWISE GRAIN

Hip to Be Square: Checking the Grain and Blocking the Fabric

Your fabric has probably traveled a long way to get to your home, and all those fibers may have shifted around. Fabric isn't perfect—it can "lean" a certain way if it's been pulled on or washed, which means the warp and weft fibers might not meet at a right angle. (And, as I said before, this can result in puckered, saggy, seriously messed-up clothes.) So, how to remedy the situation? You'll need to make sure the warp and weft yarns are squared. This is called "blocking." The first step in blocking is to find the crosswise grain. You can do this by either "ripping" or "threading."

FINDING THE CROSSWISE GRAIN
Ripping (for most light- to midweight fabrics)
Lay the fabric flat, making sure the top and bottom raw edges are straight. Clip a notch at the selvage edge and tear a thread across. The tear will rip across the crosswise grainline. Do this *slowly* and carefully or you might rip up the fabric.

Threading
If the fabric is too thick to rip—or if you are scared—just make a clip with your scissors and pull the threads off with your fingers.

BLOCKING
Once you've located the grain, fold the fabric with the selvage edges meeting. The edges should align, forming squared corners. If they don't, then the grain is off. Unfold the fabric and pull diagonally at the corners to fix it up.

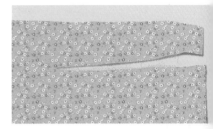

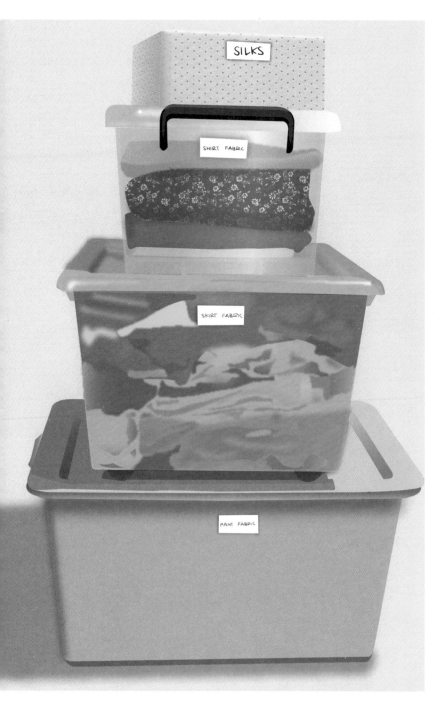

Once the fabric has been blocked, it's ready to be cut. If you are not ready to cut it yet, fold the fabric carefully and put it in storage. My favorite technique: Separate fabrics by their designated use—for pants, for shirts, for tees, and so on—and place each group in its own box. To keep track of what you have, clip a swatch of each fabric and tape it onto card stock. Punch holes in the cards and put them in a binder. This way you can easily reference your fabric collection without having to drag out and rifle through the boxes. You can even use a small binder to take with you to the fabric store if you're looking for something to complement what you already have.

BUTTONS

come in millions of different sizes and shapes. Be creative with them—the buttons you choose can really have an impact on the look of your finished garment. You might even consider using mismatched or vintage buttons. Always buy a few more buttons than you need—they get lost easily and can fall off your garment with normal wear.

EXTRA CREDIT
TRIMS AND NOTIONS

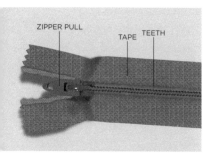

ZIPPERS

are found in different tooth sizes and lengths. For the projects in this book, we will mostly work with a seven-inch regular skirt/pant zipper. An invisible zipper is very thin and has colored teeth; it's designed to be nearly invisible. These are better for drapier, more delicate fabrics. However, depending on the look you're after, you might want the zipper to show—it can be a design element in itself.

TRIMS

This category is almost endless: There are millions of decorative elements that can make a plain garment exciting. Fabric stores sell trim, but you can also go to a trimmings store or check out www.mjtrim.com, one of my favorite Web sites. Plus, your unwanted knickknacks and fabric scraps can become trim—use your imagination! Most trims are either topstitched onto a garment or stitched to a piece's seam allowance and sandwiched between seams.

APPLIQUÉS

are decorative patches that can be hand- or machine-sewed anywhere you like. You can even make your own—simply cut out any piece of fabric in any shape you want. Iron fusible interfacing to the wrong side of the fabric shape to make it more sturdy. Pin and topstitch

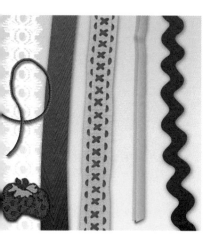

the appliqué to the garment using a tight zigzag stitch. Many store-bought appliqués come with fusible backs and finished edges, so all you have to do is edge-stitch around the appliqué to attach it to the garment.

PIPING

is a trim sewn along seam lines for a neat, outlined look.

FRINGE

comes in a variety of lengths and materials. It's not just for rodeo shirts!

LACE

can be sewn into seams or hand-stitched onto a garment for a romantic twist. Antique lace is, in my opinion, more beautiful than most of what you'll find at the fabric store. Check out vintage stores, eBay, or even Grandma's linen closet, and always cut lace off old garments before you donate them to the Salvation Army. You can also make lace insets, which look kind of like appliqués, but the fabric behind the lace is cut out so you can see through the patch.

TAPES AND RIBBONS

have a myriad of uses. You can sew them down the side of a pant leg, across the sleeve of a shirt, along the waistband of a skirt...Try doubling them up or playing with color and layout variations.

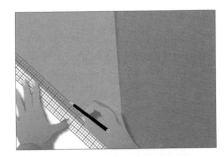

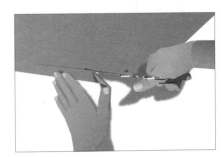

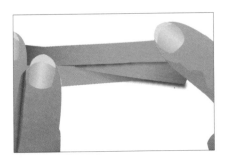

BIAS BINDING

is a strip of fabric used to finish a raw edge of a garment, such as a sleeve or neck edge. You can use matching fabric or a contrasting fabric—even a wild print to spice up a neutral-colored garment. The material is cut on the bias (at a 45-degree angle from the selvage) so that it can be sewn to curved edges easily.

To make bias binding:

1. FOLD THE TOP EDGE of your fabric to meet the selvage, forming a 45-degree angle.

2. CUT STRIPS OF FABRIC on this bias angle.

3. USE A BIAS TAPE MAKER or press it yourself by folding the strips in half and pressing,

4. THEN, FOLDING IN THE RAW EDGES, press again to make a clean finish. Or you can leave the edges raw for an interesting look.

Buy a clear plastic hanging shoe bag and keep different types of trim in each compartment. You'll be able to see what you have at a glance, and the compartments will keep everything separate and untangled.

Put zippers in zip-closure plastic bags and label them by size so you don't get them mixed up.

For buttons, take one of each kind you have and tape them into a small notebook. Take it with you to the fabric store; that way, if you find fabric you like, you'll know right away if you already have buttons to match.

STORAGE IDEAS

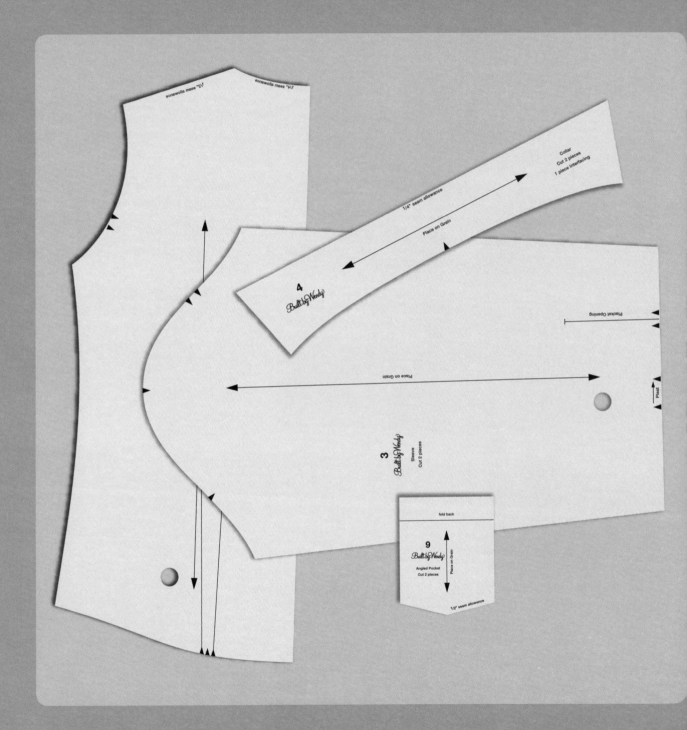

1/4" seam allowance

1/2" seam allowance

Collar
Cut 2 pieces
1 piece interfacing

1/4" seam allowance

Place on Grain

4

Built by Wendy

Placket Opening

Place on Grain

Pleat

3

Built by Wendy

Sleeve
Cut 2 pieces

fold back

9

Built by Wendy

Place on Grain

Angled Pocket
Cut 2 pieces

1/2" seam allowance

CHAPTER 3
PATTERN BEHAVIOR

What They Are, How They Work

LISTEN UP!
WHY PATTERNS MATTER

Wouldn't it be nice if all you had to do to make a shirt was, say, slice a couple of armholes into a square of fabric and call it a day? (It would certainly make my life simpler.) But if that were the case, clothes would hang like curtains. That's where patterns come in: They're the templates that help you turn a flat piece of fabric into a three- dimensional design that fits your body. Every piece of clothing you own, from your favorite old T-shirt to your most elaborately draped silk party frock, began life as a pattern. They can be tough to wrap your head around, but here's the nice thing: Once you have a basic pattern that fits you, you can make a few tweaks and come up with a totally different design. That's what this book teaches you to do. Chapters 6, 7, and 8 walk you through the process of altering the basic skirt, shirt, and pants patterns to change the sleeves or pockets or length, a procedure called pattern-making. But before you get to the creative part, it's crucial to learn how patterns work and what you'll be doing when you tweak them, and to familiarize yourself with the lingo. Pay close attention—it may seem tricky, but, as they say, you can't run without learning to walk first.

HALF-LIFE
WHY PATTERNS LOOK LIKE THAT

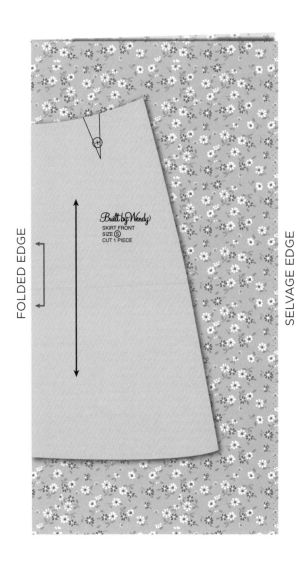

FOLDED EDGE

SELVAGE EDGE

Built by Wendy
SKIRT FRONT
SIZE (S)
CUT 1 PIECE

Patterns work on the half, meaning that each major piece of a pattern looks like only half of a garment. This half piece is pinned to a double-folded piece of fabric to ensure the garment will be completely symmetrical. When you cut, depending on the piece, you'll end up with either two identical pieces or one symmetrical piece with the fabric fold running down the center. Either way, you'll save time and effort.

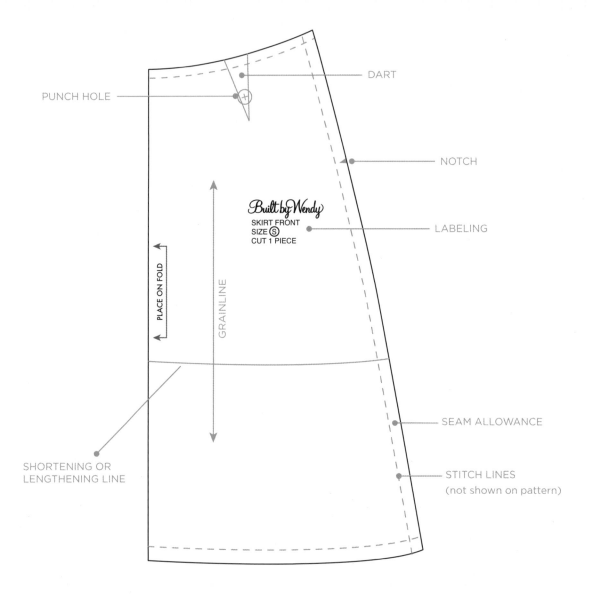

DART

PUNCH HOLE

NOTCH

Built by Wendy
SKIRT FRONT
SIZE Ⓢ
CUT 1 PIECE

LABELING

PLACE ON FOLD

GRAINLINE

SEAM ALLOWANCE

SHORTENING OR
LENGTHENING LINE

STITCH LINES
(not shown on pattern)

ANATOMY LESSON
THE COMPONENTS OF A PATTERN

GRAINLINES

Grainlines on patterns are arrows pointing in one direction or another. The grainline should run parallel to the selvage edge of your fabric.

SHORTENING AND LENGTHENING LINES

These are horizontal lines on the pattern where you can either fold (to shorten) or slash and spread (to lengthen) the pattern to make it longer or shorter, depending on the look and fit you're after. To slash and spread, you'll simply tape a piece of paper underneath the slashed pattern and extend the seam lines between the pattern pieces.

LABELING

Each pattern piece in this book is labeled with the piece name, number of pieces to cut, size, and style name.

SEAM ALLOWANCES

When you sew, you're not just running your needle along the cut edge of the fabric. Most patterns include seam allowances: a small addition in overall width to the pattern, generally around $3/8''$ to $5/8''$ on commercial patterns, which is the difference between where you cut the fabric and where you sew the seam (which will be inside the cutting line). The seam allowance will take the form of extra fabric on the inside of the seam when you're done sewing. These built-in seam allowances need to be taken into consideration when measuring a pattern against your body measurements. The seams can be trimmed down after sewing, depending on how bulky they get. I am not a big fan of doing this, and I think $5/8''$ seam allowances are too big. They're annoying to sew, especially around curves. For the patterns in this book, seam allowances are $1/2''$ on most seams and $1/4''$ around small, curved areas like necklines. See each individual pattern provided for exact seam allowances.

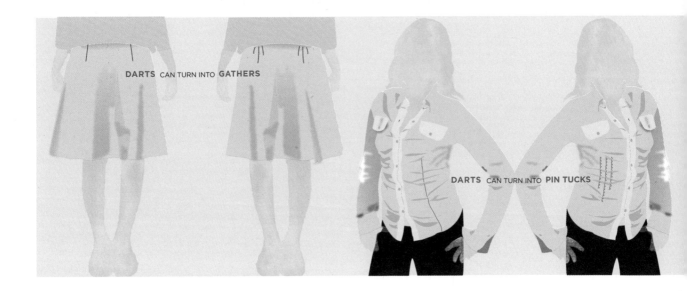

DARTS CAN TURN INTO GATHERS

DARTS CAN TURN INTO PIN TUCKS

SHAPERS

The trickiest thing about making women's clothing is their curves. Designers have to turn flat fabric into a 3-D shape, and they do this on the pattern through the use of seams, shaped seams, and darts. Seams are the stitched lines that bind two pieces of fabric together. We can alter their shape (usually by making a curve) to make the fabric fit differently. Darts are tucks sewn into the body of the garment to create contours and dimension where fabric would otherwise hang straight. On a pattern, they look like pie slices, and each line is called a dart leg. The same function can also be served with other techniques, each of which has a different look: gathering, yokes (extra panels of fabric), pin tucks, pleats, and extra seams. When you're customizing your clothes, look at where the darts and seams are on the pattern, and try to imagine other ways of creating contours. There are limitations, based on fabric weight, as to where you can change darts. For instance, on denim you can turn darts into a yoke or another seam, but the fabric is too heavy for gathering. Also, you must consider the design of the fabric when changing the contours—pin tucks would throw off the look of a large, geometric print.

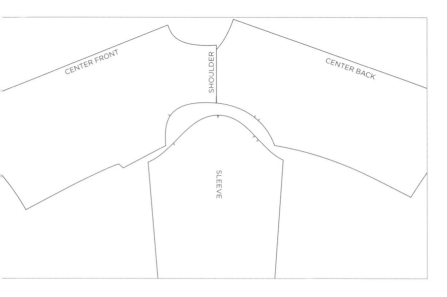

PUNCH HOLES

These are, well, holes. I like to create them using an awl. Simply press the awl into the fabric through the pattern to create a hole. Some uses:

* Mark pocket placement.

* Mark where a dart ends—the point at which the dart legs meet.

* Mark any other placements. Just make sure these punch holes will be covered.

NOTCHES

Notches are small diamond-shaped marks placed along the edges of the seam allowance. After you have cut out your pattern piece in fabric, take the tip of your scissors and cut a ¼" deep cut in the center of the diamond-shape notch, cutting through fabric and pattern at the same time.

Here's what they do:

* Mark where seams are to be sewn together.

* Mark where the legs of a dart begin.

* Mark gathering points, such as the point where the two folds of a pleat meet.

* Mark front and back pieces: Usually, a double notch (two notches placed ¼" to ½" apart) signifies the back. So, on a shirt, for instance, there will be a single notch marking the armhole for the front piece and a double notch marking the armhole on the back piece. Then, on the sleeve cap piece, which is sewn to both the front and back armholes, you'll find both single and double notches. Simply line up each type of notch and you'll know where to sew the pieces together.

TIP

Always place punch holes within an area that will be covered by sewing. For instance, there should always be a ⅛" seam allowance on the punch hole to mark the end of a dart.

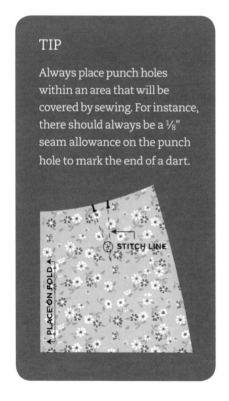

MEASURE FOR MEASURE

SIZING YOURSELF UP

MEASUREMENT CHART

	XS	Small		Medium		Large	
Size	0	2	4	6	8	10	12
Bust	31½"	32½"	33½"	34½"	35½"	37"	38½"
Waist	24"	25"	26"	27"	28"	29½"	31"
Hip	35"	36"	37"	38"	39"	40½"	42"

To determine which size you are for our patterns, you must measure three specific points: bust, waist, and hip. Because this is a beginner-friendly book, I don't get much more detailed than that, since we are simply creating some basic wardrobe pieces. If you can find a friend to help you with this, all the better—that way you can make sure your measuring tape isn't off-kilter.

It's not uncommon for women to be one size on top and another on the bottom—in fact, it happens more often than not. For shirts, the most important measurement is your bust; for skirts and pants, it's the waist and hip measurements. Use these to determine your sizes for each of the three garments.

BUST
Measure around the fullest part of your bust.

WAIST
Measure your natural waist—the smallest part of your waist. You might want to tie a string around your waist first to find the accurate point.

HIP
Measure the fullest part of your hip—usually about seven to nine inches below your natural waistline.

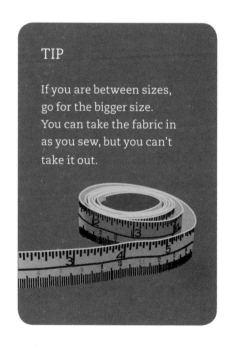

TIP

If you are between sizes, go for the bigger size. You can take the fabric in as you sew, but you can't take it out.

To Get Your Patterns Ready for Cutting:

1. UNFOLD THE PATTERN tissue paper.

2. PRESS THE TISSUE with an iron to remove any creases. Fear not, it won't catch fire—but if you skip this step, the measurements won't come out right.

3. CUT OUT ALL PIECES in your size.

4. SEPARATE THE PIECES for each style: skirt, shirt, and pants.

5. THE PIECES ARE NOW READY TO BE LAID ON YOUR FABRIC and cut out. Be careful not to tear them—they are delicate.

BBW001 SIZE K5 8,10,12   **Simplicity**

→ *Built by Wendy* →   → *Built by Wendy* →   → *Built by Wendy* →

0 39363 28117 7

Built by You

PREPARING AND HANDLING
PATTERNS

Let's Make This Permanent: Finalizing Your Favorite Patterns

If you find a pattern that suits you perfectly and you think you'll use it often, you might want to think about transferring it to a stiffer, thicker paper, such as cardboard or oak tag, so it lasts.

1. TAPE OR STAPLE the paper pattern to cardboard and cut it out.

2. TRANSFER ALL MARKINGS—notches, dart marks, punch holes, and grain-lines—using your tracing wheel. Tear off the paper pattern and redraw all the markings using your ruler and pencil.

3. LABEL THE PATTERN PIECES by name, such as collar, front, back, etc.

Out of Sight: How to Store Your Patterns

After all the work you've done to get your pattern right, you'd better not even think about stuffing it back into the tissue envelope. Imagine the tissue paper you buy for gift bags: Once you unfold it, it's never going to fit inside the plastic sleeve again. The same principle applies to tissue-paper patterns. Here are some ideas for organizing them:

For commercial tissue-paper patterns: You can iron white fusible interfacing onto the back of each pattern piece to add body and stability. Then cut out and hang the pieces in your closet using a skirt hanger with clips. Clip the envelope and instructions on too.

For cardboard patterns (see the finalizing section at left): Cut a small hole about two inches in from the edge of each pattern piece, pull a length of ribbon through the hole, and tie the pattern pieces over a hanger. Clip the style envelope to the hanger as well.

No closet space to spare? Fold your pattern carefully and place it inside an 8½" by 11" manila envelope, taping the instruction envelope to the outside. Store it in a filing cabinet.

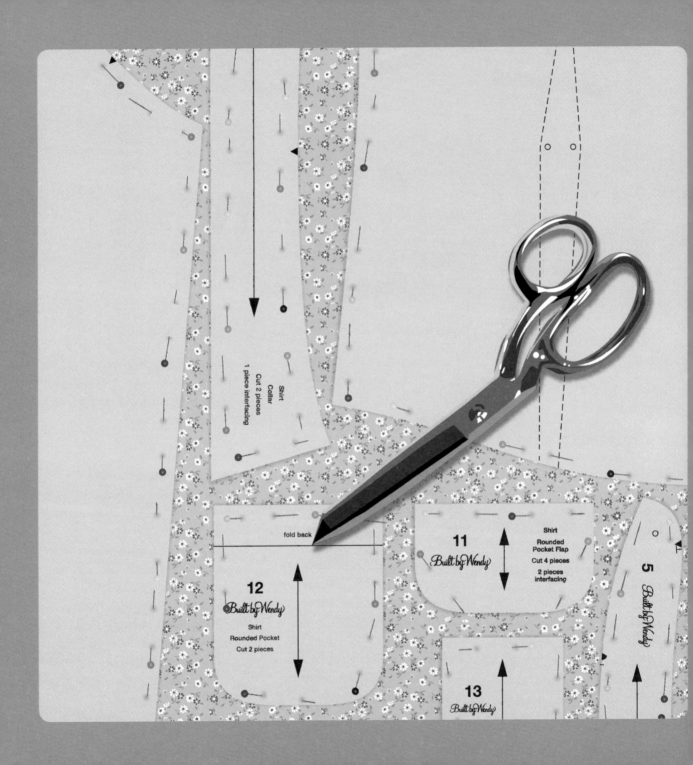

CHAPTER 4
CHOP, CHOP

Preparation and Cutting

THERE'S A SAYING IN SEWING: "THINK TWICE, CUT ONCE." I LIVE BY IT, AND SO SHOULD YOU.

The process of preparing your fabric and laying out and cutting your pattern pieces is a crucial step in any project. In this chapter, I'll show you how.

By spending the necessary time and energy on the layout and cutting of your fabric, you will:

Save time in the long run. When I first started out, I didn't have much space to cut, so I would lay out as much fabric as would fit on my table, cut those pieces, and then sew them as I cut. On several occasions, I sewed pieces out of order and had to rip some seams out and resew. Or, more often, I simply didn't have enough fabric but wouldn't realize it until it was too late. I have learned that the more time you spend preparing and setting everything up, the easier—and better looking—the finished product will be. I know, I know—we all just want to crank something out so we can wear it that night. But when I've tried to skimp or take shortcuts, the resulting mistakes caused the process to take more time, not less. The more you prepare, the less frustrating sewing will be. I promise.

Save money. If you don't think thoroughly about the layout of the pattern pieces on the fabric, chances are you'll cut something the wrong way. I've wasted more fabric than I care to remember cutting pattern pieces that should be cut "on the fold" on the selvage side (the edge), thus creating two halves instead of one whole piece; forgetting to include some pattern pieces while cutting; and cutting patterns the wrong way when the fabric had a nap (as discussed before, a texture that looks different from different angles). And if you bought the fabric a while ago and it isn't available anymore, your whole project is scrapped!

Taking Sides

Most fabrics have a right side and a wrong side—which translate to the outside and the inside of a garment. When the fabric has a print, shine, or nap, it's easy to tell the difference, but some fabric faces are subtle. If it's hard to figure out, you can check the selvage edge; the face (the right side) has a better-finished selvage edge. Or hold the fabric up to a bright light—sometimes you can simply see which side looks better. Some people prefer to use the wrong side of the fabric, depending on the style. I have used the matte side of silk charmeuse because I didn't want a supershiny garment and I liked the feel of the shiny side against my skin.

A Sense of Direction: When Cutting Is a One-Way Street

"One-way" fabrics require that every piece of a garment be cut in the same direction. This is because one-way fabrics have either a nap—like velvet, corduroy, and twill—or a pattern that is directional, such as a print with words.

It is *crucial* that you lay your pattern pieces in the same direction before you cut a one-way fabric or the results will be all mixed up. With corduroy, for instance, you could end up with different shading on the pieces that were cut the wrong way. And if you make a shirt using fabric with a directional pattern, you'd hate to have the front and back pieces pointing in different directions. I made this mistake back in college, when I decided to make some brushed-twill pants for a friend. Not realizing that the concept of nap existed, I tried to save fabric by squeezing the front and back pieces onto the one yard of fabric I had. I had to cut one piece up and one piece down. When he tried them on, I was horrified because the front looked like a completely different color than the back—the shading caused by the nap made it look much darker. I recommend cutting everything "one way" if you can; the cost of fabric is a small price to pay for the protection this will give you against messing up. In any case, always follow the directional arrows on your patterns and double-check them before you cut.

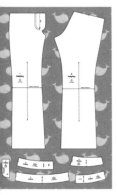

FABRIC POINTERS
TWO THINGS TO REMEMBER BEFORE YOU PLACE THE PATTERN PIECES

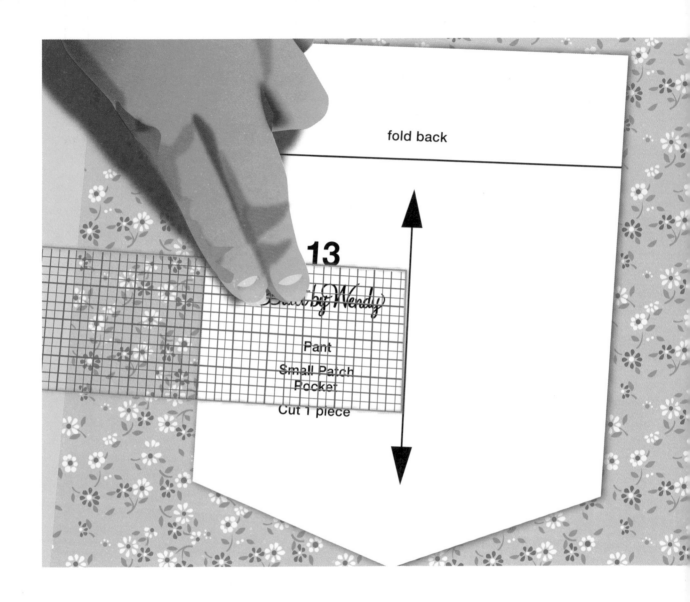

fold back

13

Pant
Small Patch
Pocket
Cut 1 piece

BY THE SLICE
BASIC LAYOUT AND CUTTING STEPS

: If you are cutting the same style and size in more than one fabric—but using fabrics that are relatively similar—you can double-layer them and cut them together. This saves a ton of time! If you're going to do this, I recommend using a rotary cutter; heavy scissors and heavy fabric can hurt your wrist.

No. 2: Patterns are mirror images. If you are cutting a sleeve on a single layer, remember to turn the pattern piece over to cut the other sleeve—otherwise, you will have two right sleeves!

No. 3: Feeling weightless? You can use other heavy things you have lying around: mouse pads, tape dispensers, three-hole punchers, pencil holders, calculators, or any desk object with heft.

Another trick: Simply tape the pattern to the fabric using painters' masking tape; you can cut through the tape, and it's easily removed without harming anything. If you prefer to use pins instead, make sure to pin within the seam allowance area to avoid poking holes in the body of the garment.

1. FOLD THE FABRIC IN HALF, selvage-to-selvage and face-to-face. The face of the fabric should be folded on the inside, so that any markings you make will be on the wrong side of the garment.

2. LAY THE PATTERN PIECES ON THE FABRIC. Try to place the pieces as close together as possible, but make sure you can fit them all in. See the individual basic pattern sections for layouts.

3. DOUBLE-CHECK that all patterns cut "on the half" are placed on the fold.

4. MAKE SURE ALL PATTERN PIECES ARE PLACED ON THE GRAIN. To do this, measure from the selvage to the pattern piece's grainline down along the grainline to make sure the line is parallel to the selvage.

5. DOUBLE-CHECK to make sure you have all the pieces laid out correctly.

6. PLACE WEIGHTS TO HOLD THE PATTERN PIECES DOWN. You can also use pins to secure the corners, but this is time-consuming. Once you get the hang of cutting, you will probably just use weights and your fingers to hold down the pieces as you cut.

7. CUT THE PIECES OUT SLOWLY and carefully—remember: "Think twice, cut once."

8. FOLLOW THE SAME STEPS FOR YOUR OTHER FABRICS, such as linings, contrast, interfacing, and so on.

Note: When cutting interfacing, you don't have to worry about grainlines, since most interfacings are not woven. You can cut the interfacing at the same time as the body piece to save time—just lay it faceup (the nonadhesive side is the face on top of the fabric but under the pattern).

ISN'T THAT SPECIAL?
LAYOUT TIPS FOR PLAIDS AND STRIPES

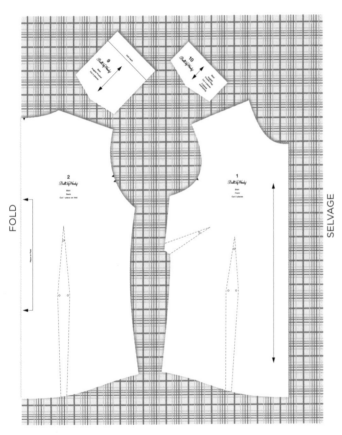

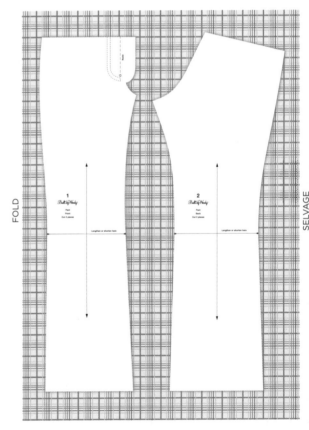

MAKE SURE PLAIDS ARE MATCHED.
Do this by laying out pieces so that the notches on the side seams are on the same horizontal plaid line.

MATCH IMPORTANT SEAM LINES.
It's difficult to match all seam lines, but the most important are the center fronts and backs of a garment, and then the side seams.

CUT DETAIL PIECES ON THE BIAS (AT A 45-DEGREE ANGLE).
Plackets, pockets, yokes, collars, and cuffs are often cut on the bias because it's tricky—almost impossible, really—to match up plaids and stripes at all those points. Plus, this adds interest to the design itself (just think of the classic cowboy shirt).

READ BETWEEN THE LINES.
Think extra carefully about stripes: Make sure that the grainlines are right for stripes, because it will really show if they are not. Also, make sure that the seams are perfectly matched up for cutting stripes on the bias—this is known as mitering—where the lines form a V shape.

Do this now, not later, because once you're sitting at your sewing machine, you won't want to get up and fix something. Mark all indicators such as notches, dart shapes, and pocket placement exactly as they appear on your pattern; that way, when you are sewing, you'll see exactly where to sew and how everything fits together.

NOTCHES

Commercial patterns generally mark notches with a V shape cut out on the seam allowance. I prefer to just snip a single $1/4''$-deep clip mark—it's quicker and easier. As a rule of thumb, single notches indicate the front of the garment and double notches indicate the back. Use scissors to clip a shallow notch through all layers of fabric.

Note: If you are putting a notch on a $1/4''$ seam allowance, be extra careful—just clip a very shallow notch. Otherwise you might cut into the body of the garment.

AFTER THE CUT
MAKING YOUR MARK

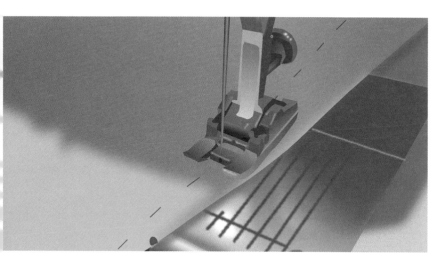

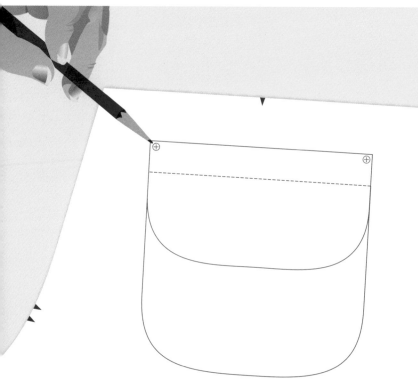

DARTS

I prefer to make notches in the seam allowance at each endpoint of the dart; I also make one that corresponds to the center point. Then I use my awl and make a punch hole in the fabric about half an inch before where the dart ends. When I am ready to sew, I just fold the dart along the imaginary line running from the center notch to the punch hole and sew; if the dart is contoured, I just kind of eyeball it. This saves time and messy marking. If you're not comfortable or experienced enough to do this, you can place colored wax paper in between the fabric and the pattern, and then use a tracking wheel to transfer the dart lines. When sewing, remember to bypass the punch hole and blend the stitch line into the dart end so as to cover the punch hole marking.

POCKET PLACEMENT

Make marks on the right side of the garment piece, $1/4''$ to $1/2''$ in from the actual pocket placement so your seams can adequately cover the markings. For a square pocket, you generally only need to mark the top corner marks. If it's a shaped pocket, you might want to mark the bottom corners too. I personally prefer punch holes, but if the fabric is delicate or sheer, you might want to mark with an erasable-ink pen.

FLORAL SKIRT WITH RUFFLE

STAYING ORGANIZED
AFTER CUTTING

If you're like me, you probably won't cut and sew on the same day, or at least in the same sitting. At my studio, I'm constantly being interrupted by the phone, and I'll often have to run out midproject to meet with buyers or suppliers, so an entire project usually takes several days from start to finish. I also find that I have more energy to focus on sewing if I take a break beforehand.

In any case, it's a bad idea to simply leave the pieces scattered around on the table. I have often had to scurry to find more fabric to match pieces I've lost and become very stressed-out in the process. (Sometimes, though, necessity can inspire you to change your design. One time, for instance, I lost the cuffs for a shirt, so I used some cotton floral napkins as fabric and recut the cuff pieces to create a very cute contrast-cuff shirt.)

Here are some tips for staying organized:

Bundling

I like to keep the paper pattern attached to the cut fabric pieces and then roll them up and tie each piece with a fabric scrap. I then put all the pieces in a clear plastic bag along with the trims and leave it near my sewing machine for when I'm ready to sew.

You can also remove the pattern pieces and rehang them together. Then stack all the cut fabric pieces into one bundle and tie. Hang this bundle on a hanger along with the pattern, or just leave it on the sewing table with the trims stuffed inside the bundle. Be sure to label the bundle with a tag listing the style information.

Saving Scraps

Tempting as it may be to toss all the fabric leftovers in the garbage, don't—you never know when you might need a scrap. Scraps get a bad rap; they're actually quite versatile. You can use them to:

* Test out thread colors and machine tension before you sew.

* Make patches.

* Make appliqués.

* Add elements to garments, such as bias binding, linings, trim, or other details.

TIP

Make a scrap chain so you always know what scraps you have in your bag. Every time you cut a new fabric, just cut off a 2" by 2" square and sew it to the end of your chain. Hang it on the wall or tie it to your chair—it actually makes a pretty cool decoration!

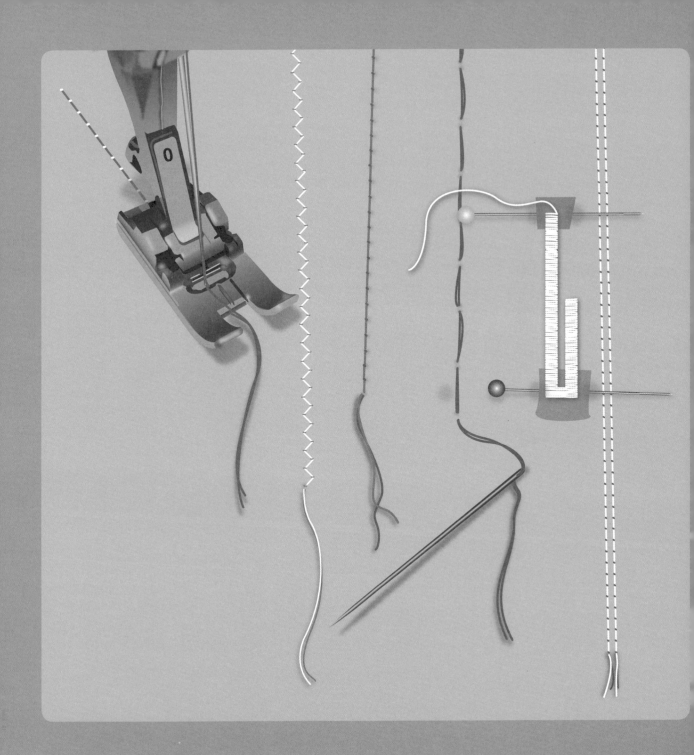

CHAPTER 5
WELCOME TO THE MACHINE

A Crash Course in Sewing

SO YOU'VE GOTTEN THIS FAR—YOU'VE CHOSEN YOUR PATTERN, CAREFULLY PREPARED THE FABRIC, AND CUT YOUR PATTERN PIECES—AND IT'S TIME TO START SEWING.

Or is it? If you're a beginner, the answer is no. Your first attempt to use a sewing machine shouldn't coincide with your first attempt to craft a pricey silk skirt. Before you sew anything you care about, you need to familiarize yourself with the machine and how it operates. It never hurts to practice first. In fact, newcomers should try the different stitches in this chapter on scrap fabric and then make a test garment (or several) to get a feel for the process and the machine itself.

When I first started sewing, I was so eager to get started that I blew off important steps like checking the tension, having all my supplies on hand, and even cutting all my pieces. I had to constantly stop to run out for buttons or to cut the interfacing pieces. (Of course, sometimes necessity can force you to get creative. Once, when I didn't have a zipper on hand for a pair of pants, I used Velcro instead for a ZZ Top vibe!)

Over the years, I have slowly built up my sewing room so that any supplies I might need are on hand—but once upon a time, I just used whatever was around. I really was the laziest sewer ever: I couldn't even be bothered to match my bobbin thread to my spool thread. I'm even guilty of having hemmed pants with duct tape! Admittedly, I still cut corners here and there, but over time I've learned what I can get away with and what never to skimp on. Because I've sewn almost every day for the past two decades, tricky skills like handling delicate fabrics and using my fingers as seam guides are second nature to me. But practice makes perfect, and making mistakes is part of the process. Stock up on cheap fabric (like muslin) and play around with it. Make all three garments in the book using fabric you don't care about. See where you mess up, take notes, and try again. Invite a friend over to watch and learn with you, and when something goes awry, you can laugh about it together. This may sound like a waste of time and fabric, but it's not—quite the opposite, in fact. Because when you suddenly find yourself in dire need of the perfect pants to wear tomorrow night, you'll be knowledgeable, relaxed, and ready to go.

Every sewing machine is different—your grandmother's hand-me-down won't look or feel like a brand-new computerized model. Read the manual carefully for specific instructions; if your machine doesn't have one, visit the company's Web site to order a new one. You should at least be able to find instructions for a model similar to yours this way. (Or, if the machine you have is a midcentury relic, you can always ask the person who handed it down to you for help. And when all else fails, Google is never a bad resource.)

Inserting the Needle

Once you've chosen the appropriate needle for your fabric, loosen the clamp and remove the existing needle. Look up from underneath: The hole will be shaped like a half-moon. You'll notice that the base of the needle also takes this shape, so match the shapes and insert the needle as far up as it will go. Then, simply tighten the clamp.

Winding the Bobbin

In most cases, your first step is to wind the bobbin, since this process generally takes place when the needle is not yet threaded. The exception: machines that have self-winding bobbins, which require you to thread the machine first and then wind the bobbin in its case. Check your manual if you're not sure.

To wind a removable bobbin, put a spool of thread on the spindle and place the bobbin on your machine's bobbin-winding pin. Guide the thread around the bobbin winder (consult your manual to locate it) and insert it through one of the holes in the bobbin. With most machines, you'll lock the machine into bobbin-winding mode and then hit the pedal. Be sure to hold on to the end of the thread for the first ten seconds or so. The winding will automatically stop when finished. Place the bobbin in the bobbin holder and guide it through the bobbin case tension spring and out the back of the bobbin case.

PREPPING
AND UNDERSTANDING YOUR MACHINE

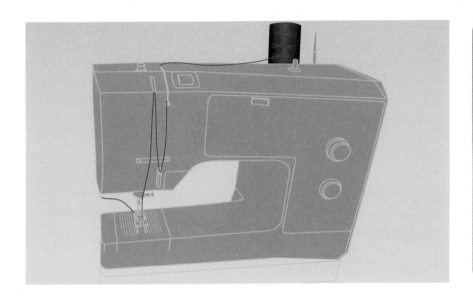

Threading Your Machine

Turn the wheel until the take-up lever reaches its highest position. Place your thread on the spindle so that it turns clockwise (or, for horizontal spools, with the notched end of the spool on the right) and carefully lead the thread through the thread guides, tension guides, and take-up lever. Don't miss a single guide, or your stitches won't happen—you'll end up with a gnarly, snarly jumble instead. Thread the eye of the needle from front to back. (Some machines thread the needle for you.) Consult your manual for instructions— some machines automatically "grab" the bobbin thread, while others require a crank of the wheel to loop the needle and bobbin threads together.

Checking Thread Tension and Stitch Length

TENSION

Each stitch is like a tug-of-war between the top (needle) and bottom (bobbin) threads. The two should link up precisely in the middle of the fabric, but sometimes one thread is pulling harder, and pulls the other to the top or bottom. If the balance is off, the result will be as mild as puckering or loose stitches—or as disastrous as a huge, unwieldy blob of thread that rips your fabric when you try to remove it. For this reason, it's essential to test tension on a scrap of your project fabric before you sew.

Fold the scrap and run a few lines of stitching. If the fabric puckers or the stitches seem loose, the tension needs to be adjusted. To find out where the problem lies, try using two very different colors in the bobbin and spool so you can see them clearly. Run some more lines and inspect the results. If you see both colors on the top side, the needle tension is too tight; if you see both colors on the back, the needle tension is too loose (or, less likely, the bobbin tension is too tight).

Generally, the needle thread is the one that will need adjusting, and this adjustment is easily done on your machine—check the manual for details. It's not recom-

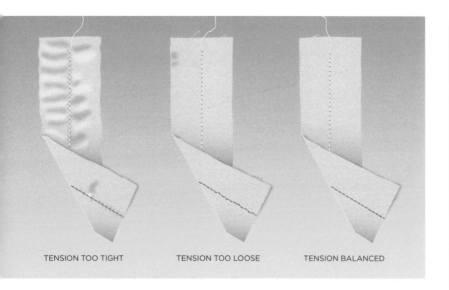

TENSION TOO TIGHT   TENSION TOO LOOSE   TENSION BALANCED

WHAT IS A STITCH, ANYWAY?

A machine stitch is formed when two threads—the needle thread and the bobbin thread—link together. The needle thread starts at the top of your machine and, as you've probably guessed, goes through the needle. The bobbin is the minispool located underneath the needle inside the machine. This you'll have to wind yourself (I'll explain how shortly), though you can buy prewound bobbins.

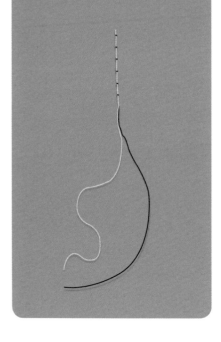

mended that you adjust the bobbin tension yourself—the bobbin tension is preset and usually works fine. Ideal tension varies depending on the fabric weight and stitch length, so make sure you're testing the same fabric and stitch length you plan to use for the project (more on that in a minute). Keep tweaking and experimenting until the balance is just right.

STITCH LENGTH

Your stitch length should be calibrated *before* you sew—not as—or different parts of the garment will look different. The standard stitch length is 2.5. As a general rule of thumb, the tighter the stitch

length, the stronger the stitch and the nicer it looks. Make sure it's not *too* tight, though, or the fabric will pucker. Stitch length settings don't necessarily indicate how long the stitches will be, because thinner and lighter fabrics move more quickly (thus resulting in longer stitches at the same setting). Use slightly longer stitches for topstitching. They look better, and since topstitching is mostly decorative, a stronger, short stitch length (which uses up more thread) is not necessary.

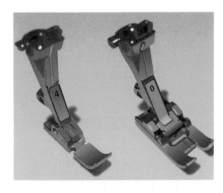

½" SEAM ALLOWANCE

Presser Feet

The assortment of presser feet out there can be overwhelming: narrow-rolled-hem feet, jeans feet, button feet...It's all too much for me. I generally just use my all-purpose sewing foot—the one that comes installed on the machine—and a zipper presser foot for when I'm sewing zippers. Sometimes I use the blind-hem foot—which creates a nearly invisible stitching line—but for the projects in this book, you really only need two, especially if you're a beginner. Have your presser feet on hand and ready to go when you start sewing.

Seam Allowance Guides

The metal throat plate around your needle hole will have several lines, which may or may not be marked with measurements. Each increment measures ⅛". The patterns in this book use a ½" seam allowance, which means that the edge of the pattern must align with the ½" allowance guide while you sew. The exception: Around small curved areas (like necks), the seam allowance is ¼". Use the edge of your all-purpose sewing foot as a guide for the ¼" seam allowances.

The Seven Commandments: A Before-You-Sew Checklist

☐ **1. CLEAN AND OIL THE SEWING MACHINE** according to its instructions. Be sure to remove lint from inside the bobbin case and under the feed dogs.

☐ **2. WIND A FEW BOBBINS** so you don't have to wind a new one in the middle of your project. All that unthreading and rethreading will interrupt the flow of your sewing.

☐ **3. DETERMINE** the best stitch length.

☐ **4. BALANCE** the thread tension.

☐ **5. SET UP YOUR IRONING BOARD AND PRESSING TOOLS,** and heat up your iron—you *must* press each seam before you get started on the next one.

☐ **6. IRON ALL FUSIBLE INTERFACINGS** to the appropriate pieces. Don't forget to use a pressing cloth or iron plate.

☐ **7. SET OUT AND ORGANIZE** all trims and notions near your sewing machine so they can be grabbed easily when you need them. Sewing can be a very Zen activity—but not if you have to interrupt yourself to tear the room apart looking for a button.

HANDS AND FEET: GETTING A FEEL FOR THE MACHINE

As you'll notice when you practice, the machine can feel as though it has a mind of its own. A small tap on the foot pedal can make it accelerate faster than a Ferrari (or so it seems). The trick is to start slowly and increase the speed once you feel more comfortable. As for your hands, you're probably wondering how hard to push the fabric. The answer: Don't. Those zigzagged metal pieces on either side of the needle hole—called feed dogs—pull the fabric in for you, so all you have to do is steer the fabric to make sure the edge matches the correct seam-allowance guide. Practice with the fabric you'll be using first, and you won't be in for any unpleasant surprises when the time comes to make your garment.

Keeping It Together: Pinning Fabric Pieces

Before you sew, it helps to pin fabric pieces together at notch points and at various points in between—as many as you need to make you comfortable—so that the layers are sewn together in precisely the right place. With enough practice, you'll be able to skip the pins and just use your fingers to hold pieces together at notches while you sew (that's what I do). Insert pins at a 90-degree angle to the seam, with pin heads facing the outer edge, and remove the pins as you sew—before the needle arrives, or you might break the needle. Be careful to pin within the seam allowance, especially if you're using thin, delicate fabric—you don't want to poke holes in your brand-new masterpiece.

Stitching and Finishing Seams and Edges

Before you start sewing, it's important to understand that there are several kinds of stitching, with vastly different uses, stitch lengths, and placements. And remember: When you stitch seams, you also have to finish seams to prevent fraying. The two go hand in hand.

Here is the order in which you'll stitch:

1. Stay-stitching is a special stitch for prepping fabric.

2. Joining seams to stitch pieces together.

3. Finishing seam allowances is important to prevent the raw edges from unraveling.

4. Outer stitching, such as edge-stitching and topstitching, is done on the outside of a garment to secure shape or for decoration.

5. Finishing edges is the final step; you'll need to close off raw edges that do not meet to form a seam, such as hems and armholes.

SEWING
A CRASH COURSE

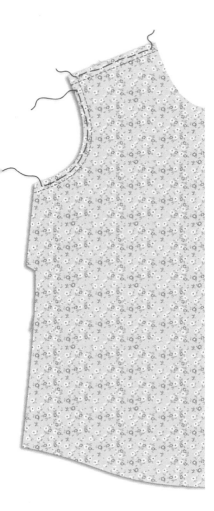

1. Stay-Stitching: Your Insurance Policy

A stay stitch is not a seam—it's a stitch you make on a single layer of fabric before you join seams. Corners, curved seams, and any area sewn on the bias (such as shoulders) tend to stretch out while sewing. A quick, easy line of stitching inside the seam allowance will keep them in shape and save you the frustration of having to deal with saggy, baggy garments.

As a reformed slothful sewer who once hated prep work, I have often blown off stay-stitching. Of course, I learned my lesson the hard way. I once made a narrow-shouldered blouse with puff sleeves out of very expensive Sea Island cotton batiste. I tried it on to find that the shoulders were all stretched out, and my perfect puff sleeves slumped over the shoulders like a dowdy secretary blouse. I had to add some awkward, time-consuming pin tucks into the shoulders to make them slimmer. If only I had stay-stitched!

To stay-stitch, sew a straight stitch $1/4''$ to $1/8''$ from the edge of the fabric—as long as it's within the seam allowance. Feel free to use a looser stitch length, since it's not going to show.

TIP

Shoulders can be tricky to stay-stitch. Sometimes it's easiest to sew a piece of securing tape along the length of the shoulder to prevent it from stretching out. Or you can cut a thin strip of fabric along the lengthwise grain (which is the strongest grain, the one that doesn't stretch out) and add it—or a strip of stabilizing tape—to the seam. To do this, pin the front and back shoulder pieces face-to-face. Just before sewing the seam, place the piece of fabric or tape on top and stitch it down at the same time. Sometimes you can slip the tape through the wide hole in your presser foot so that the tape is constantly being stitched on top of whatever you are sewing.

2. Joining Seams

Make sure the tension is correct, you're using the right needle, and your bobbin and spool are well stocked. Align the pieces so that the outer edge corresponds to the appropriate seam allowance measurement. Don't forget to stitch forward and then backstitch to secure the line of stitching. Then, off you go!

TIP

Feeling shaky? A magnetic seam guide is an attachment you can buy to form a barrier along the correct seam-allowance guide—which means your fabric can't move past it. This will help your seams stay in line.

Beginner's Corner

Exercise 1: A Simple Plan for Stitching a Seam

1. PULL OUT A FEW INCHES OF THE TOP THREAD AND BOBBIN THREAD, and place them behind the presser foot.

2. PLACE TWO PIECES OF FABRIC UNDER THE RAISED PRESSER FOOT, using the seam-allowance guides to indicate where the edge of the fabric should stay.

3. LOWER THE PRESSER FOOT.

4. USE THE HAND WHEEL TO START THE FIRST COUPLE OF STITCHES. Hold the threads up while you do this and make sure there are at least a few inches of thread trailing. If you don't, the threads might get sucked under—and that will suck, because you'll need to rethread the needle.

5. STITCH FORWARD ABOUT A HALF INCH, then stitch in reverse (check your machine's instructions if you can't figure out how) to secure the beginning of the seam. Then proceed forward. (You do not need to backstitch if you're merely stay-stitching.) When you reach the seam's end, stitch back and forth about half an inch to secure the threads, then clip them off, preferably with small scissors, near the fabric (but please don't cut the fabric). That's it!

Sewing and Finishing Darts

The dart is a pie-shaped mark on the pattern that usually has subtle shaping in the "dart legs" to create a concave or convex shape. Darts must be sewn *before* the body of the garment is joined at the seams.

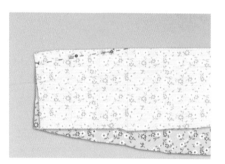

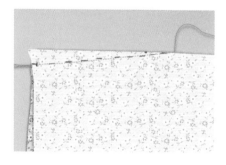

To sew a dart:

1. LAY THE PATTERN PIECE on the wrong side of the fabric piece.

2. USE A TRACING WHEEL and wax paper to mark the shape of the dart leg. (After years of practice, I sometimes just eyeball it.)

3. FOLD THE DART in half and pin.

4. SEW WITH SMALLER STITCHES (stitch length 1.5 or 2 on your machine) up the dart leg from the outer edge in the direction of the center of the fabric piece. Bypass the punch hole by half an inch until you reach the dart point.

5. DO NOT BACKSTITCH to end the dart as you would a regular seam. Instead, snip and tie the loose threads in a knot.

6. PRESS THE DART TO ONE SIDE. Because darts are so narrow, it's not necessary (at least with these patterns) to cut them open and finish them.

Excuse Me, Can I Ask for Directions? Which Way to Sew Seams

As a rule of thumb, it's best to sew from the widest part to the narrowest part of a garment piece, or follow these specific guidelines:

Shoulder seams. Sew from shoulder to neck.

Side seams. Sew from underarm to waist.

Skirts and dresses. Sew from hem to waist.

Pant legs. Sew from hem up side seam, and from hem to crotch. Still not sure? Look closely at the broken seam-allowance lines on your pattern. They have tiny arrows indicating the sewing direction.

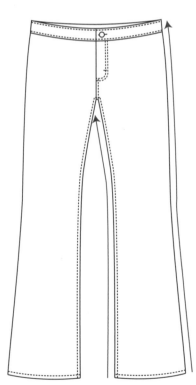

Dangerous Curves: Dealing with Contoured Seams

Curved seams help clothing fit your body perfectly, but sewing-wise, they are (pardon the pun) a bit of a curve-ball. That's why you'll need special tricks to handle them. In any curved seam, one piece of fabric will curve inward and one will curve outward. Because of this, the seam allowances will cause trouble once the seam is sewn. On the inward curve, it will bunch up, and on the outward curve, it will be stretched. The solution: Get out your shears. Once you've done a stay stitch on each piece just inside the seam allowance, clip (for inward curves) or notch (for outward curves) at regular intervals from the edge to the stay stitch. This will create space for over-lapping fabric on the inward curve, and open up space on the outward curve.

Pressing is a crucial step to take after every seam you sew, but it's especially important with curved seams. Press the seam to one side using a press-ing ham if you have one (otherwise, a rolled-up towel works nicely). For a sleeve, press the cap seam toward the body of the garment.

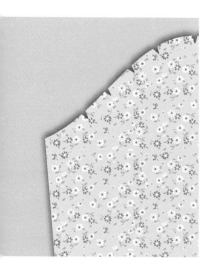

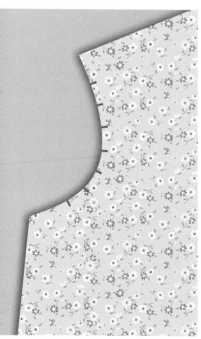

Exercise 2: Stay-Stitching, Notching, and Stitching a Curved Seam

1. USING THE SHIRT PATTERN that comes with this book, cut a piece of scrap fabric along the pattern for the shoulder area of the sleeve piece. Leave some leftover fabric below this curved cut.

2. TAKE THE FRONT SHIRT PATTERN PIECE and cut out some fabric along that curve.

3. LINE UP THE PIECES AT THE NOTCHES AND PIN. Now you'll have a small curved seam (half a shoulder) to practice with.

4. STAY-STITCH: RUN A LOOSE STITCH WITHIN THE SEAM ALLOWANCE. Careful with the curves! If you want to draw a line where the seam should go, this will help you. Use your clear ruler to mark dots, then connect them with a pen or marker.

5. TIME TO NOTCH AND CLIP. On the piece that curves inward (concave), use your shears or small scissors to create simple clips from the edge to the line of stay-stitching. On the piece that curves outward (convex), create V-shaped notches.

6. SEW THE SEAM AND INSPECT THE RESULTS. Any bunching? Keep trying until you get it right.

3. Finishing Seams

If all you do is sew your seams, turn the garment right-side out, and call it a day, your garment might be okay—that is, until you wear it around for a day. The unfinished edges could fray like crazy, and, depending on the fabric, this will (a) ultimately weaken the garment; (b) show through the fabric, making you look like a slob; and/or (c) tickle. The solution is to finish the seams, and there are a myriad of methods to do this, depending on the fabric. (Necks, waists, bottom openings, and sleeve openings need to be finished with facings, collars, or waistbands, but we'll get to that a bit later.) Right now, I'm referring to the inside of the garment, such as the side seam of a skirt—for obvious reasons, you don't want those seams unraveling during normal wear. The best way to finish your seams is to use an overlock (serger) machine, but those are expensive, so unless you're a serious sewer, you might want to pass on buying one. There are all sorts of elaborate ways to finish seams (turned-under seams, French seams, hand-overcast seams), but for the sake of simplicity, I'll go over just my favorite quick, easy techniques:

PINKED EDGES. Use your pinking shears to trim the seam edges. This is the fastest, simplest method and will prevent most tightly woven fabrics from unraveling. Press the seam open when you're finished.

ZIGZAG STITCH. I recommend doing this if your fabric is loosely woven or noticeably fray-prone. Depending on what makes sense for the location of the seam, you can either press the seam open and run a zigzag stitch down each seam allowance, or press the seam to one side and zigzag-stitch the seam allowances together.

SEAMS GREAT. This is an ultrathin folded fabric tape that wraps easily around raw edges to bind them with less bulk than regular fabric. Simply topstitch it on and you're all set.

PINKED EDGE

ZIGZAG

SEAMS GREAT BINDING

4. Outer-Stitching

Once your seams are joined (in other words, you've stitched the pieces together on the inside of the garment) and finished, you sometimes need to do other stitching on the outside of the garment, either for decorative purposes or to secure the shape (pressing doesn't always do the job). You'll be doing this on plackets, collars, cuffs, waistbands, pockets, and flies, to name a few places.

EDGE-STITCHING. This stitch, which uses very small stitch length, can hold down interfacing or serve as a decorative topstitch. As its name suggests, it's placed right at the edge of the seam—sometimes less than $1/16$" away! Because it is much finer and closer to the edge than the usual $1/4$"-wide topstitch, it results in a dressier look.

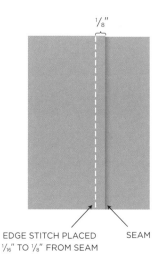

EDGE STITCH PLACED $1/16$" TO $1/8$" FROM SEAM — SEAM

BAR-TACKING. You can use this stitch to secure areas that get a lot of wear, such as belt loops, pocket corners, and flies. They are mostly used on work-wear and denim. Sometimes a metal rivet will replace a bar tack. To make: Set your sewing machine to a very tight zigzag stitch. Stitch a $1/4$" line on the outside of your garment. Try doing two lines crossed to make a cute criss-cross bar tack. It's also fun to change the thread color to make the bar tacks more decorative.

TOPSTITCHING. For a sportier vibe, use a topstitch, which is usually placed $1/4$" from the seam edge. (You can also try a double line of topstitching, which is essentially an edge stitch combined with a topstitch—two lines of stitching running parallel to each other $1/4$" apart. This technique is commonly used on jeans and sportswear.) Topstitching helps to secure seams but is also a great opportunity for you to get creative—try playing it up by using a longer stitch length and thicker or contrasting thread.

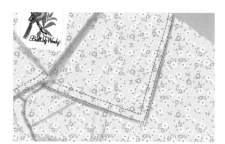

5. Finishing Edges

When all your seams are finished, you're still not finished. The final step in sewing is to cover up the raw edges of the garment, such as the waist of a pair of pants or a skirt, the hem of a garment, or the armholes and neckline of a shirt.

Necklines and waists are usually finished with collars and waistbands. Sleeves are generally finished with cuffs. But some styles don't have these pieces. Sleeveless shirts, plain necklines, and waistbandless skirts and pants are finished with what's called facing. This is a piece of fabric that faces the inside of the garment and forms a mirror image of the shape of the opening. (Have a look inside one of your sleeveless shirts and you'll get the idea.) You can also finish these openings with bias binding, a strip of bias-cut fabric that wraps around the raw edge. The bottom of a garment is almost always finished with a hem.

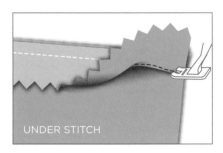

UNDER STITCH

FACINGS

Facings are generally made of the same fabric as the garment. Here's how to make and attach a facing:

1. FUSE OR STITCH INTERFACING to the facing piece.

2. FINISH THE RAW EDGE (the one that is not being joined with the body of the garment) using the turn-back method: Fold about $\frac{1}{2}''$ under (toward the side with interfacing) and simply topstitch the fold down.

3. PIN THE FACING TO THE GARMENT, right side to right side.

4. STITCH THE TWO TOGETHER, leaving a $\frac{1}{2}''$ seam allowance. Clip or notch the seam allowances where necessary on curved seams.

5. PRESS THE RESULTING SEAM ALLOWANCE toward the facing.

6. UNDER-STITCH. This is an edge stitch you'll run on top of the seam allowance near the facing edge, thus securing the seam allowance to the facing side and eliminating bulk.

7. TO PREVENT THE FACING FROM FLIPPING OUT, you'll need to secure it inside the garment. You can do this by hand-stitching the facing to a shoulder seam or side seam. Or you can use your machine's blind-stitch function to secure the entire facing to the body. (This is a bit time-consuming but looks clean.)

TIPS

No. 1: Some designs call for facing to be sewn with its right side to the wrong side of the garment, so the facing ends up on the outside of the garment as a decorative element. It then gets topstitched down to the garment—you can even insert some piping first!

No. 2: Bias binding can be made out of any fabric, so use your imagination— try different prints, stripes, plaids, and metallics for extra contrast. You can also sandwich all sorts of trim into the bias binding, so try slipping in some piping or even a tiny ruffle or two.

BIAS BINDING

We've gone over this before: Bias binding (also known as bias tape) is a strip of fabric that wraps around a raw edge to finish it. You can buy it at the store, but sometimes it's more fun to make your own if you feel like getting creative.

Store-bought binding already comes with its edges folded over, so simply slip your garment's raw edge inside the folds of the binding and edge-stitch it. Start and finish at a seam—that way, the binding seam will be less conspicuous.

Homemade binding is made using a bias tape maker (one of my all-time favorite inventions) or by carefully measuring and cutting a 1"-wide strip of fabric along the bias. Prepare it by pressing the strip in half vertically, then folding in the raw edges. Then insert your raw fabric edge into the folded binding piece and edge-stitch.

TIP

A quicker way to work with home-made bias binding is to cut the bias strip and sew the raw edge of the strip to the raw garment edge, right side to right side.

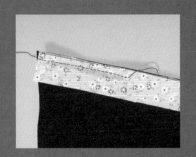

A. Use your presser foot as a seam guide (which creates a ¼" seam allowance).

B. Then use your fingers to fold back the binding, and you'll see a nice, even ¼" finished edge with the raw edges hidden.

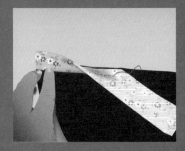

C. On the back side, use your fingers to fold the raw edge under to create a clean, even ¼" finish.

D. Press it down, pin it, and edge-stitch.

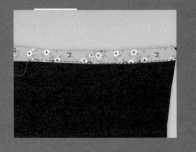

Bottoms Up!
How to Sew Hems

The thickness of a garment's hem depends on several factors: the shape of the hem, the fabric type, and how you want it to look. No matter what type of hem you're sewing, one thing is crucial: You must measure and press it carefully. Keep your clear ruler at hand and make use of it. Check and recheck to make sure the line isn't sloping at an angle, and try the garment on before you sew.

Exercise 4: Creating a Hem

1. TAKE A PIECE OF SCRAP FABRIC at least a few inches wide, of any length you wish—it's good to have at least half a yard or so to play with because you'll have to stitch for at least that long when you're working with the real thing.

2. FOLD BACK THE RAW EDGE BY $1/2$" AND PRESS. Try pulling the fabric from the sides to make this easier.

3. FOLD THE PRESSED EDGE UNDERNEATH ITSELF BY 1" so that the raw edge is hidden under the fold. Press.

4. PIN AT SEVERAL POINTS ALONG THE "HEM." Then run a stitch about $3/4$" from the finished edge. You can do this wrong side up if it's easier to see what you're doing. Try doing it right side up— topstitching—once you've got the hang of it.

5. TRY MORE DIFFICULT, SMALLER HEM HEIGHTS: Fold back $1/4$" and then $1/4$" again, and run the stitch $1/8$" from the edge (which is an edge stitch).

6. TRY AN EASED HEM: Cut out a triangular shape of fabric instead of a square. You'll notice that the fabric of the hem is wider than the finished edge of the right side. Use pins to spread out this difference rather than creating a bubble of extra fabric at one end.

SHIRT HEMS

On a shirt, you generally don't want your hem to make much of a statement—the idea is for it to look delicate and small (especially if you'll be tucking it in; chances are, you're *not* looking to add volume to your abdominal area). One-quarter inch is the standard shirt hem thickness. My shirt pattern has a $1/2$" hem allowance, which means that once it's folded under itself and sewn, it finishes at $1/4$".

1. Fold up the hem $1/4$" and press.

2. Fold the hem over on itself another $1/4$" and press. Place pins throughout if you're a beginner. Measure and try the garment on to make sure the hem is perfectly even.

3. Topstitch just under $1/4$" around so you are catching the edge of the hem on the inside. If it makes you more comfortable, stitch with the wrong side of the garment facing up.

EASE, PLEASE

When you're sewing a hem on a garment with a flared shape, the folded part of the hem might be slightly longer than the body of the garment—envision what will happen if you try to fold an A-line skirt and you'll get the idea. The folded underside won't move as quickly as the single-layer garment body, and there's more of it, so it's going to bunch up no matter what. If you don't spread the extra bulk evenly across the hemline—"ease" it, in sewing jargon—it will all show up at the end of the seam, with nowhere to go.

The solution is to pin carefully. Pin the hem at all seam lines and at several other points around the hemline, allowing for a small amount of ruffling to occur all around the folded underside. Sew slowly and carefully, and give the folded part a bit of a push if it's moving too slowly. If this sounds scary to you, practice on leftover fabric first.

GOING BLIND: THE INVISIBLE STITCH
(Beginners, Beware)

Many professional tailors use what's called a blind stitch to finish hems. This can be done by hand or machine and it looks just like it sounds, which is to say it doesn't look like anything: Only one out of every few stitches pricks the outer surface, so no stitching lines are visible. It makes for a cleaner, more professional look, especially if you're working with suiting or other extrafine fabrics. That said, I'm not a huge fan; I think it can get easily messed up, and the folding process is tricky.

Some machines come with a blind-hem foot, or you can buy one and attach it yourself (just make sure your machine is able to do zigzag stitches).

SKIRT HEMS

Skirt hems typically fall somewhere in the range between $1/2$" and 2". The general rule is that thicker fabrics have wider hems, and vice versa, but it's really up to you—inspect some of the skirts you already have to get an idea of the look you like. For a casual canvas skirt, for instance, you might go with $1/2$", unless you want a thicker hem as part of your design (this could be accented with a contrasting thread color). For a light, silky fabric, I suggest a small $1/4$" hem so that the fabric can flow freely. For a thick wool skirt, on the other hand, a wide 2" hem is easier to fold and sew, reduces bulk at the bottom, and emphasizes the fabric's sturdiness. My skirt pattern has a $1 1/2$" hem allowance, which finishes at a good all-purpose width of 1". Feel free to play around with it, but here are the guidelines for the 1" hem:

1. FOLD BACK THE RAW EDGE $1/2$" and press.

2. FOLD UP AGAIN 1" and press.

3. DOUBLE-CHECK YOUR MEASUREMENTS, then press, pin, and topstitch or blind-hem around about $3/4$" from the bottom edge (see Try This on page 99).

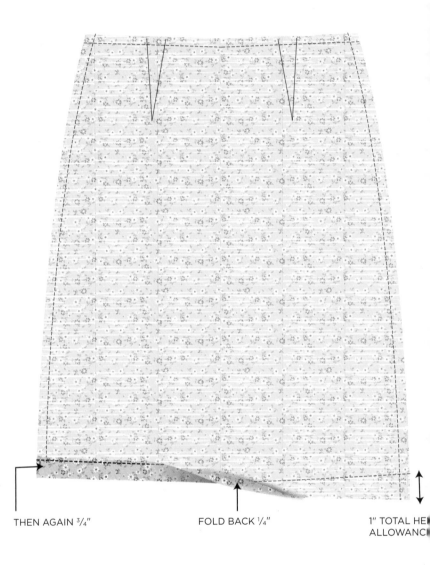

THEN AGAIN $3/4$"   FOLD BACK $1/4$"   1" TOTAL HE[M] ALLOWANC[E]

THE BOTTOM LINE

My skirt patterns come with hem allowances, but every body's different—so save yourself the trouble of rehemming or lengthening, and decide on the actual hem height yourself. This is much easier to determine when you have another person helping you (as you can probably imagine, the hem height you pin when you bend over won't look the same when you're standing up straight). Put on the shoes you'll be wearing with the garment, make sure the waist is hitting you in the right spot, and stand up straight. Have your friend measure from the floor to hem height at points around the skirt using a yardstick, and mark using tailor's chalk or pins. Remove the skirt, measure to make sure the line is even, and use that line as your fold-back point.

PANT HEMS

Pants generally have a 1″ hem allowance that finishes at a $^3/_4$″ hem. For jeans, the hem width is usually $^1/_2$″, but for nicer fabrics like wool suiting, you might want something a bit more polished-looking: say, a 2″ hem using a blind-hem stitch. Pant hems aren't as visible as skirt hems, so your options are more varied in terms of finish. You can fold the 1″ hem halfway back and then fold it beneath itself again for a $^1/_2$″ clean finished edge. Or you can fold the 1″ hem back only once for a wider hem and finish the raw edge with binding or even pinking shears if you're feeling lazy.

TIPS

No. 1: If you want to make any of these hems wider than the allowances built into my patterns, simply tape a piece of paper to the edge of the pattern and use your eighteen-inch clear ruler to extend the hemline.

No. 2: Skirts cut on the bias must be hung on a clip hanger overnight before measuring and hemming, because the weave will stretch out in different places.

TRY THIS!

A topstitched hem can look pretty casual. If that's not the style you're after, you might want to attempt the blind-stitch hem, or even apply lace hem trim instead. If neither of those options appeals to you, keep in mind that a smaller stitch length will look dressier.

Pressing

You must, must, *must* press each seam after you sew. It will make your project look far more professional, because once a seam is joined to another seam, its fate is sealed. Some pieces, like collars, must be pressed because you need to turn and top-stitch before you attach it to the body of the garment. Here are my time-tested pressing tips:

* Always use a press cloth, unless you're working with linen or cotton (which is not so heat sensitive).

* Always press on the wrong side of the fabric. Heat can alter the surface of the fabric, causing it to shine.

* Iron in the direction of warp (the strongest grain) so the fabric doesn't stretch out. Be gentle.

* To avoid steam circles from the iron, use a nonsteam iron and spray water directly on the fabric.

* Place a piece of fabric under the garment so the heat is conducted better.

* Use a piece of fabric to cover small pieces with stitching like cuffs, collars, and plackets so you don't smush the seams.

The Finish Line: How to Sew Notions

When I started sewing, I wanted to keep things as simple as possible. One of my first pieces was a gathered-waistband skirt. I didn't know how to put in a zipper—nor did I feel like learning—so I cut an elastic waist-band and then bunched up the skirt fabric haphazardly to sew onto it. From there, I advanced to a pink cotton twill jumper—basically a more elaborate version of the gathered skirt. It had over-the-shoulder straps that were supposed to button shut. I was a bit overwhelmed by the thought of buttonholes, however, so I just cut slits in the fabric and secured the raw openings with clear nail polish. My cute buttons would cover the holes anyway, or so I figured. (Well, they did—that is, until the holes ripped.)

The point is, I understand that buttons and zippers—especially zippers!—can seem scary. But, as with anything else in sewing, patience and caution are the keys to getting them right. Here I've simplified the techniques as much as possible.

ZIPPERS

There are two common types of zipper applications: centered (in which the zipper has equal amounts of fabric on either side) and lapped (in which the seam allowance on one side creates a flap to hide the zipper). For simplicity's sake, I focus here on the centered-zipper technique; it's much easier, and a good way for beginners to learn. The patterns in this book can use a regular seven-inch zipper (available in many colors) or an eight-inch invisible zipper (for skirts only), which is designed to be nearly invisible from the outside of the garment and requires a special invisible-zipper foot that you'll have to buy. If you're a beginner, do yourself a favor and start with a regular zipper.

Centered-zipper application for skirts

1. SEW THE CENTER BACK SEAM up to the notch point as marked on the pattern. This is where the zipper will end.

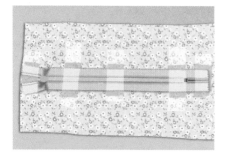

2. CHANGE YOUR MACHINE'S STITCH length to the longest setting (5) and machine-baste the seam from this point to the top edge.

3. FINISH THE SEAM ALLOWANCES along the center back seam. Press the seam allowances open.

4. PLACE THE ZIPPER FACEDOWN on the pressed-open seam allowance. Carefully check to make sure the zipper is aligned perfectly with the center seam. The top of the zipper should hit $1/2''$ below the top raw edge.

5. TAPE THE ZIPPER TO THE SEAM using regular clear tape or special basting tape. Place a pin beneath the bottom stopper of the zipper so you know where to start stitching.

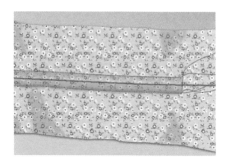

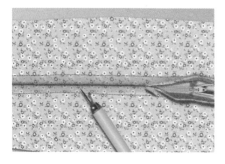

6. REMOVE THE PRESSER FOOT from your machine and insert the zipper foot. Turn the skirt over, and topstitch $1/4''$ away (the width of the zipper foot) on each side of the seam, starting from the bottom on each side.

7. STITCH A HORIZONTAL LINE beneath the end stopper to connect the stitching lines on each side. Be sure not to hit the end stopper or you'll break your needle.

8. CAREFULLY REMOVE THE BASTING STITCH from in front of the zipper using a seam ripper, and the tape from the back side.

Jean fly zipper application for pants

This process is a bit more complicated than the one for skirts, but I will show you an easy way to do it in chapter 8 (Pants).

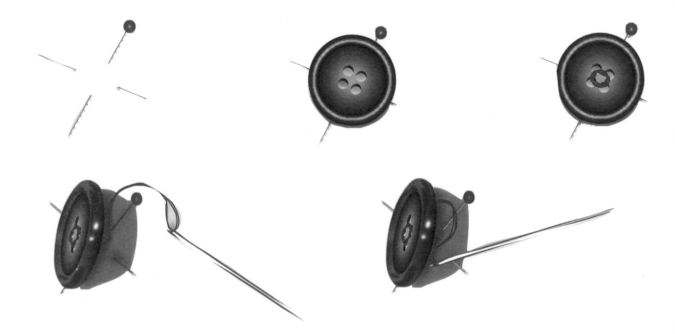

BUTTONS AND BUTTONHOLES

The most common excuse I hear from my terrified novice friends: "I can't even sew on a button!" Well, here's how. Buttons are available in a dizzying variety of colors, shapes, and sizes—and even without visible holes (known as shank buttons)—but they all go on essentially the same way.

Attaching buttons

Keep in mind that if a button is sewn on too tightly, it'll have an awfully tough time wiggling through the hole. You need to give it some space and create a shank—basically, a stem of wrapped thread—so the button can move around without snapping off.

1. PLACE TWO PINS CRISSCROSSED where the button will lie to create some space between the button and the garment. Then position the button and tie the thread through the holes at least three or four times.

2. REMOVE THE PINS. Wind the thread around itself a few times in the space beneath the button. This will create a shank for added strength and flexibility.

3. BRING THE THREAD THROUGH to the wrong side of the fabric. Stitch a couple of times to secure, then knot the loose threads and clip.

TRY THIS!

Mix up thread colors for contrast, or stitch diagonally across the holes to make an X design.

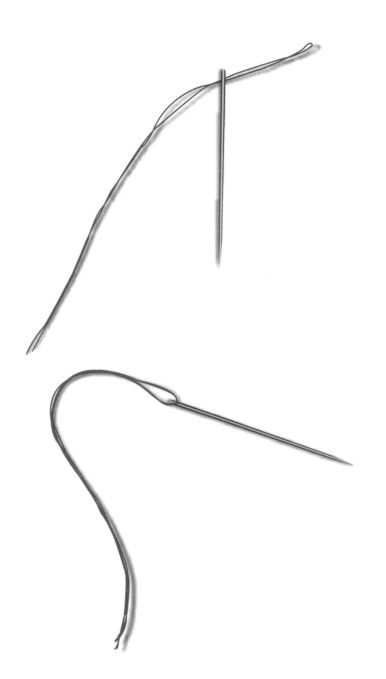

Threading needles

I hate hand-stitching, but it's the only way to attach buttons. Luckily, it's a pretty simple process. To save yourself the hassle of having to stitch through the button many times, it's easiest to double-thread your needle, creating a thicker thread.

1. CUT A LENGTH OF THREAD. If you're not sure how much you need, try about eighteen inches.

2. FOLD THE THREAD IN HALF and thread the folded tip through the eye of the needle (you might want to use a large-eyed needle and a threader for help).

3. KNOT THE LOOSE ENDS (four threads). I knot them at least twice.

TRY THIS!

Buttonholes don't have to be a bore. Try using a contrasting thread color for buttonholes or changing up the layout. I personally like a double-button layout.

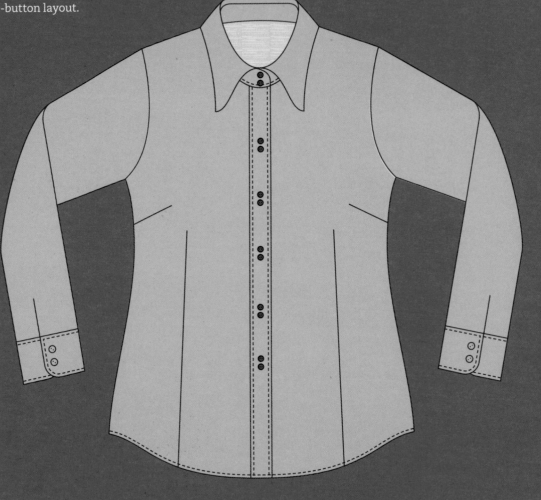

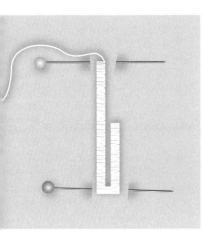

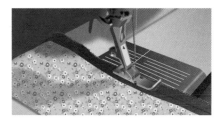

If you don't have a buttonhole function on your machine, you can create buttonholes using a zigzag stitch.

1. MARK THE DESIRED LENGTH of the buttonhole with pins on each end.

2. SET YOUR MACHINE to a tight zigzag: stitch length 0 and stitch width 2.

3. STITCH TWO ROWS VERTICALLY between the pins, leaving about $1/8''$ of space in between. Then stitch a horizontal bar tack at top and bottom to connect the vertical rows.

4. SNIP THE HOLE—BE CAREFUL!— and finish with clear sealant or nail polish.

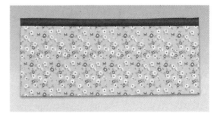

Buttonholes

Hopefully, your machine has an automatic buttonholer; most modern versions do. Set the length that will cover your button size—the hole should be $1/8''$ longer than the button. Make sure the placket where you are making holes has interfacing attached—otherwise your holes will look rumpled and puckered. If you're going to be varying the button layout, measure extremely carefully. Mark the locations first using your clear ruler, making sure the buttonholes are at even intervals and centered perfectly. Start with the bottom buttonhole—mistakes won't be as obvious there. Place the needle at the top of where the opening will be, and the machine will work its way down. Then fold and gently snip the hole, finish with sealant or even clear nail polish, and voilà!

> ### TIP
>
> If you decide to use buttons that are bigger than the holes marked on the pattern, you must increase your buttonhole size. Your buttonhole should be $1/8''$ larger than your button.

PIPING, SEAM TRIMS, AND TAPES

When sandwiching piping, fringe, or lace between two pieces of fabric in the seam allowance, I like to use my zipper foot so I can really get close to the edge. I recommend doing this in two steps for maximum accuracy and strength: Stitch the trim to the face on one side. Then place the other piece on top, pin the pieces together, turn the whole thing over, and stitch right over the previous stitch line.

To attach tape, simply pin it where you want it and edge-stitch it to the garment.

CHAPTER 6
SKIRTS

THE BASIC SKIRT IS A BIT LIKE A TRIANGLE WITH THE TOP CUT OFF—ALL YOU NEED TO FORM ONE ARE TWO SIDE SEAMS, A WAISTBAND, AND A HEM. FOR THIS REASON, IT'S THE SIMPLEST PLACE TO START.

When I was a beginner, I made skirts all the time because they were such a fun and easy canvas to customize. Before I knew how to work with zippers and waistbands, I would take a rectangular piece of fabric, stretch a band of elastic along one side, and sew it to the fabric using a zigzag stitch. This resulted in a dirndl-style gathered-waist skirt—not exactly the most flattering look for a high school girl, especially when I made one in thick 14-wale corduroy (which didn't gather too well).

I also went a bit overboard with decorations; once, I remember, I stitched a Technicolor assortment of buttons all over the body of a skirt. It looked cool—or so I thought at the time—but I cringed with discomfort the second I sat down. Still, it wasn't a total waste of time: In fact, all of my mistakes ultimately helped me to figure out what works and what doesn't.

In this chapter, we'll work with the pattern pieces for a basic A-line skirt—a universally flattering shape that can take on a million permutations. I'll walk you through four different projects, from an airy summer skirt to a tweedy, collegiate-inspired version. But bear in mind that these are only starting points. You can make all sorts of simple alterations to the basic patterns and the project tickets, not only by changing up fabrics and trims, but in other ways that affect a skirt's fit and overall aesthetic: the waistline, the body shape, and the hem height. Just keep practicality in mind; after all, you don't want to take too many chances with the bottom half of your body. How high is too high? Do you want to accentuate the waistband or will you be wearing the skirt with long tops that will cover the waist? Can you sit in it? Do you need a lining? Do you want belt loops? Would a slinky fabric hang more beautifully with an extra-flared shape? Would thick, slightly stretchy wool be perfect as a pencil skirt? Consider when and where you'll wear your skirt, and then start designing!

Difficulty Level: Easy

Sewing Skills Needed: Joining seams, finishing seams, hemming, zipper insertion, sewing darts, under-stitching

PATTERN PIECES

CUTTING

The way you lay out your skirt pattern pieces will depend on the fabric you use: napped fabrics are laid out differently than two-way fabrics, and stripes must be mitered to meet in precisely the right place. Note that detail pieces and linings are not included in these layout maps—I've only shown you the basic skirt. Buy extra fabric to cut out the detail pieces—and to cover your mistakes!

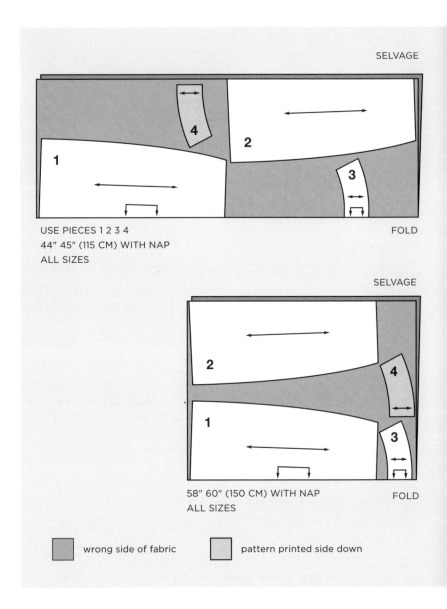

USE PIECES 1 2 3 4
44" 45" (115 CM) WITH NAP
ALL SIZES

58" 60" (150 CM) WITH NAP
ALL SIZES

wrong side of fabric   pattern printed side down

SEWING YOUR SKIRT

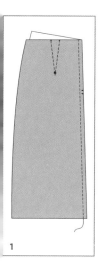

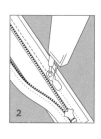

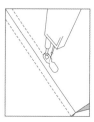

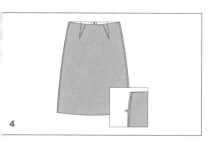

1. CENTER BACK. Pin the back skirt pieces face-to-face, then sew the center back seam from the hem up to the dot notch (where the zipper will begin, if you're using one), then baste-stitch the seam up to the waist. Finish the raw edges of the center back and press the seam open.

2. ZIPPER. Use a zipper foot. Open the zipper; place it facedown on the extended seam allowance so that the top stop is $^{3}/_{4}$" down from the top edge and the teeth are centered on the center back basted seam. Baste the zipper along the guideline on the zipper tape. Close the zipper and baste the other side. Turn the garment over and topstitch $^{1}/_{4}$" around. Remove the basting from the center back seam to open the zipper.

3. DARTS. Sew the front and back darts. Press the darts toward the center of the garment. You can also baste with tape (see page 101).

4. SIDE SEAMS. Before doing this, stitch on any pockets if that is part of your design. Pin the front piece to the back piece—face-to-face—along the side seams. Stitch them together, finish the seams, and press them open.

5. FACING. Attach the interfacing to the facing. Pin the front facing to the back facing (or the lining to the lining) face-to-face. Stitch the side seams together, press them open, and finish the bottom edge. Stitch the facing around the skirt's waist. Turn the facing out, press the seam allowance toward the facing, and under-stitch the seam allowance to the facing. Turn back the facing's raw edge above the zipper. Fold the facing down inside the skirt and press. Tack the center back facing to the zipper tape. You can also stitch it down following the zipper stitch line that is there already. Tack the side seams of the facing to the skirt's side seam allowances to secure—or you can blind-stitch the entire facing to the body of the skirt.

6. HEM. Fold the hem to the height desired, press in the raw edge $^{1}/_{4}$", then stitch along the edge.

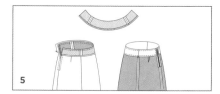

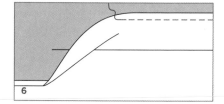

The Waist

ELASTIC OR DRAWSTRING WAIST

This results in a sportier, more casual look—the kind of skirts you'll toss on for the beach or a Saturday afternoon of shopping. If you'll be making this type of waist, *do not sew the darts.* This will result in a more generous waistline, leaving room for the drawstring to do its job. And here's some good news: You don't need to sew a zipper or facings, since the skirt just pulls on! Finish the top raw edge and fold it back 1″. Then topstitch it down, leaving 2″ open to insert an elastic or a drawstring.

For elastic

I suggest a ¹/₂″-wide elastic—just make sure it is the right color. In other words, if your skirt is white, don't use a black elastic, because it will show through.

Cut the elastic according to the size chart below. Attach a safety pin to one end of the elastic to hold it in place, and push it through the tunnel—try a loop threader to make it easier. Once the elastic is pulled through, sew the ends together, making sure the entire piece lies flat: Place one end on top of the other and stitch back and forth a few times. Finish by closing the 2″ opening.

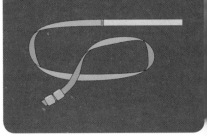

TRY THIS!

If you want the look of a drawstring and the comfort of an elastic waistband, try a combination: Cut a piece of elastic about 18″ long, then attach a piece of drawstring (about 20″ long) to each end. Feed this through the drawstring holes in the center front of the skirt waist.

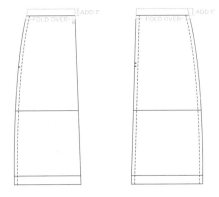

	XS	S	M	L
Cut elastic	19″	20″	21″	22″
Cut drawstring	58″	60″	62″	64″

BUILT BY YOU
SKIRT DESIGN IDEAS

For a drawstring

Make two small buttonholes 1½" down from the center front top edge. Fold back the hem 1" and topstitch. Insert the cord through the buttonhole, and pull through. If you're feeling creative, try tying beads at the end of the cord.

BIAS BINDING–COVERED WAIST

You don't have to use the waist facings provided. Instead, you can quickly and simply cover the edge with bias binding. Try using a contrasting fabric, or cut an extralong strip of binding, which you can tie in the center back.

WAIST WITH OUTSIDE FACING

Instead of having the facing flip toward the inside of the garment, why not use it as a detail on the outside? Just be sure to reverse the rules: Sew the right side of the facing to the wrong side of the skirt. Then flip it over and topstitch it down. You can use an entirely different fabric, contrast stitching, piping, or other trim to make this functioning part of the skirt's finish into a design accent itself.

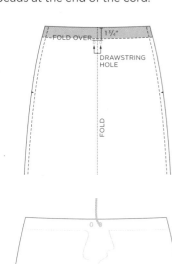

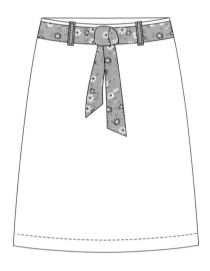

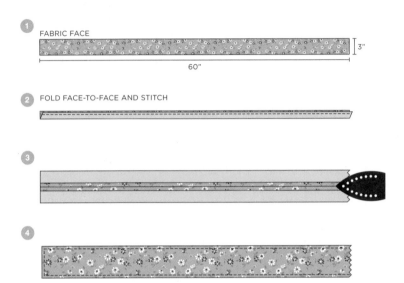

1 FABRIC FACE

3"

60"

2 FOLD FACE-TO-FACE AND STITCH

3

4

SELF-BELT AND BELT LOOPS ON WAIST

Make a self-belt (a belt made out of the same fabric as the skirt) or one in a contrasting fabric.

To do this:

1. CUT A RECTANGLE OF FABRIC that is 3" long by 60" wide down the length of the fabric—in other words, along the selvage.

2. FOLD IT IN HALF, FACE-TO-FACE, and stitch a $1/2$" seam allowance.

3. MOVE THE SEAM TO THE CENTER, press it open flat, fold the ends inside for a finished edge, and press.

4. TURN THE TUBE.

5. TOPSTITCH EVENLY around the entire belt.

Make the belt loops as shown in chapter 8 and stitch them on. I would suggest two in the back, two on the sides, and two in the front. Use your clear ruler and mark the placement for the top and bottom of each belt loop to ensure even distribution. You might want to make the belt hang lower on the hips; that way, it'll be more visible if you're wearing a longer shirt. To do this, simply place the loops lower—this works especially well if you've put facing on the outside, in which case you'll attach the belt loops to the facing. In any case, be sure you wait until the facing is complete before attaching the belt loops!

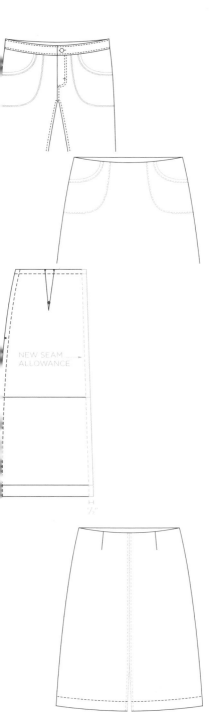

The Body

POCKETS

Try using the pockets provided for the pants in chapter 8. They can be sewn and placed onto skirts in the same ways.

SEAMS

You can add seams anywhere you want, whether the goal is function or fashion—just make sure you also add seam allowances to the pattern or you'll swallow up an inch of fabric that you might not be able to afford to lose! For instance, you can add a center front seam with a slit.

To do this:

1. TAPE PAPER to the straight edge of the center front pattern piece.

2. USING YOUR 18" CLEAR RULER, mark a $1/2$" seam allowance along the front edge. Cut this paper part out and use this expanded pattern piece when cutting the fabric.

3. WHEN SEWING THE PIECES TOGETHER, stop before you get to the bottom—this will be the slit. Press the seam open and edge-stitch down each side of the seam. It's a good idea to reinforce the slit; add a tiny topstitch back and forth horizontally where the opening begins.

PROJECT IDEA

Try cutting the two front pieces in a striped pattern so that the lines are mitered (meeting in a perfect V). This can be tough for beginners, but it's an interesting challenge for more experienced sewers. And, well, it looks cool.

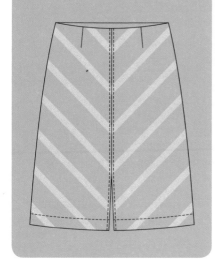

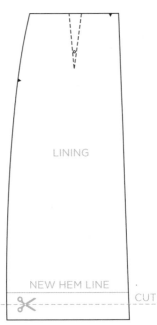

LINING

NEW HEM LINE

CUT HERE

LINING

Yeah, I know: Linings seem scary. But all you're doing, essentially, is making facing pieces that go all the way down. Lining pieces are mirror images of the pattern pieces, except that you need to skim about one inch from the hem length so that the lining doesn't hang out. If you need to line a skirt, simply cut out the front and back pieces in lining fabric (or any friction-free fabric you want, really). Keep in mind that if you're using lining, you don't need facing.

Sew the skirt together, and then sew the lining together the same way, leaving the center back part open for the zipper. Sew the skirt and the lining face-to-face around the waistline and turn the lining to the inside of the skirt. Sandwich the zipper in between the skirt and the lining when you sew it.

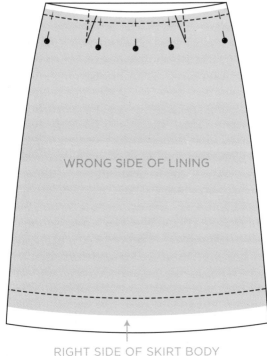

WRONG SIDE OF LINING

RIGHT SIDE OF SKIRT BODY

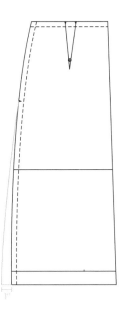

SHAPING THINGS UP: A-LINE VS. NARROW CUTS

You can skim the side seams to make this pattern less A-line, or add width so that the skirt flares out more. Just a few things to keep in mind:

* Make sure the new side seams meet your hem at right angles. Otherwise, the hem will meet in a point or inverted point, and that looks unprofessional.

* Always work from the hip notch down, blending the new side seam to that point. The pattern is designed to fit your hips—the widest part of your lower body—and if you tweak anything above that point, you'll mess with the fit.

* If you make the skirt very narrow, you'll need to add a slit so you can walk.

A-line

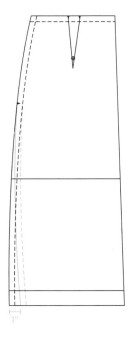

To make a skirt more A-line, tape paper to the side seams of the front and the back pattern pieces. Add the amount you want to each piece, working from the hip notch down and making sure the additions are symmetrical. If you simply want a wider skirt, I'd start by adding $3/4$" to $1^1/2$" to each side seam. This will add 3" to 6" total to the circumference of the skirt hem.

Pencil skirt

To make a slim skirt, skim off anywhere from $3/4$" to $1^1/2$" (from the hip notch down). Don't go overboard! Remember, you might need to add a slit to the center back or side seams so you can walk. If you feel like it, you can insert a zipper into the slit.

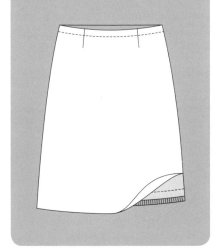

TRY THIS!

Why not add fringe or lace trim to the lining piece so that it hangs out from the skirt slightly? Or use brightly colored lining fabric for (hidden) contrast. Only you will see it, but isn't that the fun part?

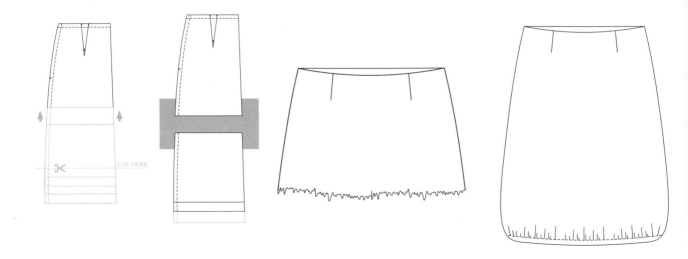

The Hem

The hem of a skirt is a great place to add details such as trims and ruffles. You can create an almost infinite variety of styles without having to deal with complicated sewing.

SHORTENING AND LENGTHENING

If you are shortening or lengthening the skirt by only a few inches, you can either fold or spread (see chapter 3) at the shortening/lengthening lines on the pattern pieces. This will keep the bottom opening measurement the same. But if you want to make a miniskirt or a full-length skirt, it's best simply to remove or add length following the shape of the hem, using your clear ruler for guidance. Don't forget to include the hem seam allowance in your measurement.

TRIMS

Trim can be easily topstitched around a hem, so go out and find one that inspires you! Try beaded trim on a velvet skirt, leather trim on a plaid wool skirt, a floral trim on a corduroy skirt, or a rainbow of rickrack on a cotton twill skirt. And keep in mind that trim doesn't have to form a straight line around the bottom: Try mixing things up by stitching diagonal strips along one bottom corner. You can cover the hem with bias binding or even insert elastic inside the hem to make a bubble skirt. These are all easy ways to add color, detail, and excitement to a basic piece.

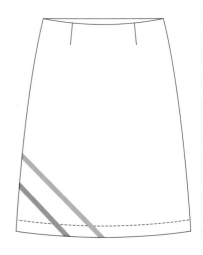

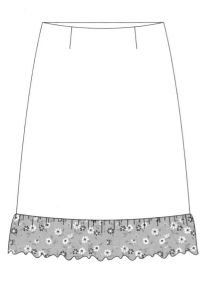

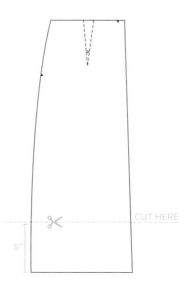

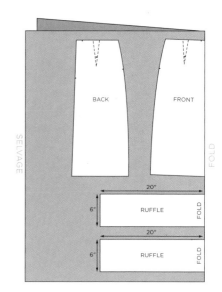

RUFFLES

You can make a basic skirt into a tiered bohemian skirt or a prairie skirt by skimming a few inches off the hem and replacing that section with a gathered piece.

Here's how to do it:

1. USING YOUR CLEAR 18″ RULER, measure up from the hemline (on both the front and back pattern pieces), following the shape of the hem, 5″ above. Use points to mark the line, and connect the points. The cutting line for the hem is at this new line.

2. MAKE A RECTANGULAR PATTERN piece that is 6″ long and 20″ wide.

3. PLACE THIS PIECE ON THE FOLD and cut it twice.

4. USING A BASTING STITCH, sew two rows ¼″ apart in the seam allowance. Pull the lower thread to gather the piece, and spread the gathers evenly. Pin the ruffle equally along the skirt hem, and sew this piece to the body piece.

5. REMOVE BOTH ROWS OF BASTING stitches.

You can play with the ruffle height and skirt length to achieve a variety of effects. You might try covering the hem with decorative tape to emphasize the ruffle.

Congratulations!

Now you know a few easy techniques to make a cool, detailed, not-boring-in-the-slightest skirt. I've created four options, which I'll walk you through, but feel free to tweak these ideas as much as you like. Filling out a project ticket for each skirt you make will help you to keep track of what you need and what is optional.

BUILT BY YOU

PROJECTS

SKIRT PROJECT TICKET

STYLE:

TRIM NOTES:

FABRIC AND TRIMS:

PATTERN NOTES:

SEWING NOTES:

Project #1:
The Summer Skirt

This is a white handkerchief-linen drawstring skirt with a long ruffle hem and white satin trim around the ruffle. You can also use other colors o types of trim—try making the skirt in a lightweight, brightly colored cotton with rickrack trim for a south-of-the-border look. Instead of satin, you can use fringed trim, or the type with little dangling fluffy balls (very sailing-in-Santorini). Or just make the skirt plain and use a tropical floral print.

SKIRT PROJECT TICKET

STYLE: SUMMER SKIRT

TRIM NOTES:

* 1/4" white elastic — 1 yard
* white pony beads — 4
* white cotton cord — 1 yard
* 1/4 wide white satin tape — 2 yards

PATTERN NOTES:

* remove length off skirt
* make ruffle for hem
* make skirt front and back top edge wider so it can fold over for drawstring

SEWING NOTES:

* do not sew front and back darts
* do not sew zipper — sew closed the entire back seam
* fold over top edge and fill tunnel with the elastic/cord drawstring
* finish drawstring with pony beads
* add ruffle to hem and cover seam by topstitching on satin tape

FABRIC AND TRIMS:

white linen

FRONT VIEW

BACK VIEW

SKIRT PROJECT TICKET

STYLE: BACK-TO-SCHOOL SKIRT

TRIM NOTES:
* black leather piping (1 yard)
* small black leather shank buttons (2)
* black fusible interfacing for facings
* green lining (1 yard)
* black 7" regular skirt zipper

PATTERN NOTES:
* add 3" to length
* cut facing in contrast
* cut body in wool plaid and in lining
(skim 1" off hem of lining)

SEWING NOTES:
* sew facing to outside
* insert piping in facing
* edgestitch facing to body
* fully line

FABRIC AND TRIMS:

plaid wool

for contrast facing

lining

FRONT VIEW

BACK VIEW

Project #2:
The Back-to-School Skirt

This is a plaid wool skirt, cut on the bias, that hits midcalf. It has a solid-color facing sewn onto the outside with piping and two buttons, and is fully lined. You can also make this out of striped fabric and make the facing in a contrast-print fabric.

Project #3:
The Holiday Skirt

This is a black velvet skirt with fringe-trimmed lining and sequin and beaded appliqués topstitched on to form a design. You can also make this in cotton twill decorated with thin colored tapes.

SKIRT PROJECT TICKET

STYLE: HOLIDAY SKIRT

TRIM NOTES:

* silver sequin trim (8 yards)
* black lining (1 yard)
* black 7" regular skirt zipper
* black 2" long fringe
* floral shape satin appliqué

PATTERN NOTES:

* add 1" to length
* cut body in velvet and in lining (skim 1" off hem lining)

SEWING NOTES:

* topstitch sequin trim to body
* topstitch appliqué to front
* topstitch fringe to lining

FABRIC AND TRIMS:

black velvet

black lining

FRONT VIEW

BACK VIEW

SKIRT PROJECT TICKET

STYLE: PREPPY SPRING SKIRT

TRIM NOTES:

* 7" navy zipper

PATTERN NOTES:

* shorten to mini length — no hem allowance needed to be included since we are covering the edge with bias binding
* use rounded patch pockets
* don't use facings
* cut contrast bias binding

SEWING NOTES:

* use bias binding around hem, pocket edges, and waist edge

FABRIC AND TRIMS:

indigo denim

contrast for bias binding

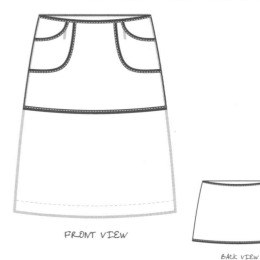

FRONT VIEW

BACK VIEW

Project #4: The Preppy Spring Skirt

This is a cotton canvas miniskirt with patch pockets and floral-print bias binding around all the raw edges—very Palm Beach in feel. If you're not planning on sipping Arnold Palmers at the country club anytime soon, mix up the fabric and bias binding for a totally different effect: Use black cotton with white binding for a Mod look, or create your own combination.

CHAPTER 7
SHIRTS

EVEN IN ITS SIMPLEST INCARNATION, A SHIRT IS PROBABLY THE MOST USEFUL THING IN YOUR CLOSET.

You can wear it on its own, belt it, deck it out with accessories, or layer it underneath sweaters, jackets, or vests. It's easy to care for, it's (usually) seasonless, and it will never go out of style. And, in my humble opinion, you can never have too many. What's not to like?

As you've no doubt noticed, shirts are composed of many more parts than skirts. The bad news is that this makes shirts more difficult and time-consuming to make, but the good news is that your options for customizing and trimming a shirt are virtually limitless. Not only can you add trim anywhere, but you can remove and add pieces like pockets and epaulets. You can tweak the collar and cuffs to make the shirt more feminine. You can play with the length and shape of the sleeves or give them a puff. You can change the buttons. Essentially, you can do whatever you want—and I'll show you how.

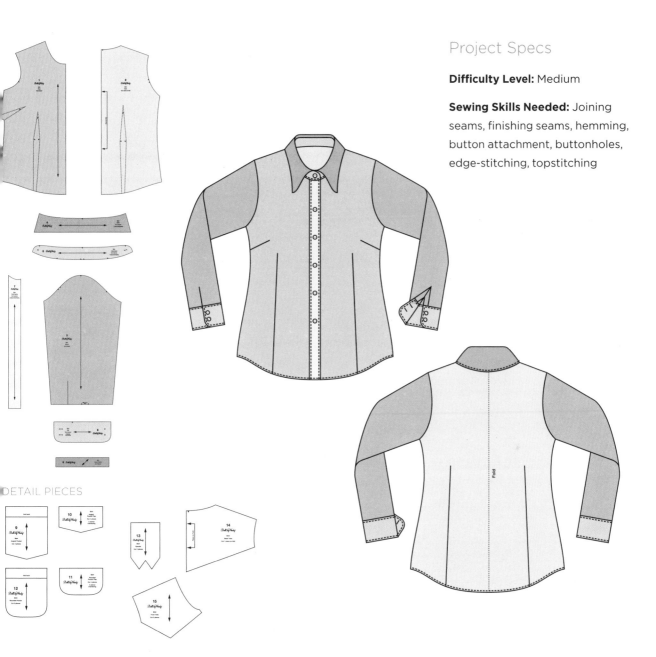

Difficulty Level: Medium

Sewing Skills Needed: Joining seams, finishing seams, hemming, button attachment, buttonholes, edge-stitching, topstitching

DETAIL PIECES

PATTERN PIECES

CUTTING

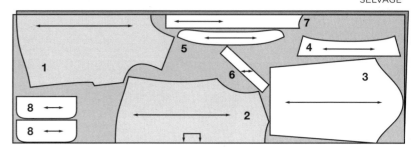

SELVAGE

USE PIECES 1 2 3 4 5 6 7 8 9
44" 45" (115 CM) WITH NAP
ALL SIZES

FOLD

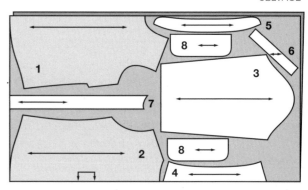

SELVAGE

58" 60" (150 CM) WITH NAP
ALL SIZES

FOLD

☐ wrong side of fabric   ☐ pattern printed side down

SEWING YOUR SHIRT

1. FUSE THE PIECES. Fuse or sew the interfacing to the collar, collar stand, cuffs, and front facing. If you are using pocket flaps or epaulets, you can also support those with interfacing.

2. DARTS. Sew the front and back darts by folding the dart in half down the center, pinning, and stitching along the dart lines. Start in the middle of the dart and stitch to each point. Clip in the middle so it lies flat.

3. DETAILS. If your design has pockets or yokes, stitch them on now.

A. For yokes: Press the back edge of the yoke, pin the piece flat to the shirt body, and stitch it down.

B. For pockets: Finish the top raw edge, then fold the top edge along the fold line and stitch down the side seam. Turn over the top edge and fold back the side and bottom edges along the stitch line. Topstitch along the top edge. Pin to the body and stitch down the side and bottom seams to the body of the shirt.

C. For pocket flaps: With the right sides together, stitch around the side and bottom edges along the seam allowance. Trim around the corners if they are bulky, turn the flap, and press. Topstitch around the edges. Baste the flap above the pocket, fold it down over the pocket, and stitch the top edge down.

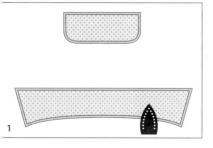

1

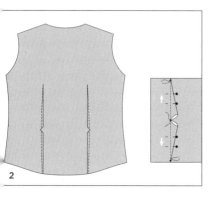

2

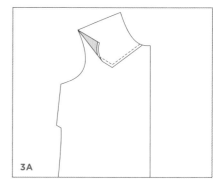

3A

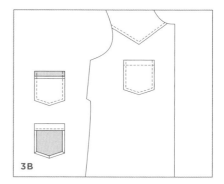

3B

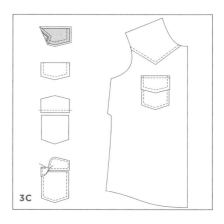

3C

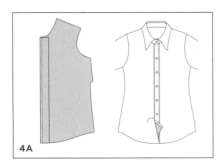

4A

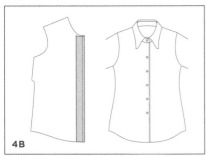

4B

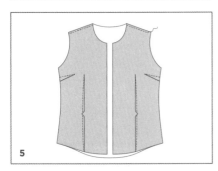

5

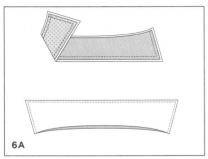

6A

4. FRONT FACING. Stitch the front facing to the front pieces.

A. Outside facing: Stitch the right side of the facing to the wrong side of the front, then fold it back to have the facing on the outside of the garment. Fold back the raw edge and topstitch it down to the front. The outside facing is a good place to insert ruffles or piping for decoration.

B. Inside facing: Stitch the right side of facing to the right side of the front. Fold back the facing to the inside of the front and stitch down the edge. The buttons and buttonholes will secure the facing in place. This is good for a cleaner look.

5. SHOULDERS. Stitch the shoulder seams together, and finish the seams.

6. COLLAR

A. With the right sides together, stitch around the collar piece. Turn the collar using your wooden point, press, and topstitch around the edge.

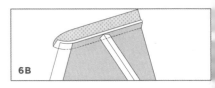

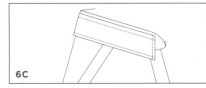

6B

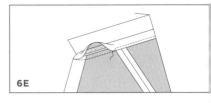

6C

6D

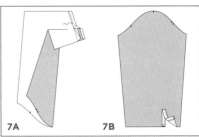

6E

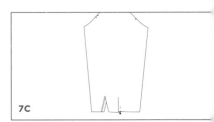

7A

7B

7C

B. Stitch the collar stand to the neck of the shirt. Press the seam allowance toward the collar stand.

C. Stitch the collar to the right side of the collar stand.

D. Fold back the raw edge of the other collar stand piece and pin the right sides together with the other collar stand, sandwiching the collar in between. Stitch.

E. Turn the collar stand, and edge-stitch around the entire collar stand.

7. SLEEVE PLACKET. To finish the sleeve placket (the slit coming up from the cuff):

A. Stretch open the placket slit to a straight line and stitch on bias binding to cover the raw edge.

B. Press so that one half (the side closest to the front half of the sleeve) is pressed back and the other half is pressed flat.

C. Fold the sleeve pleat, and pin it in place.

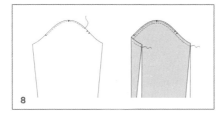

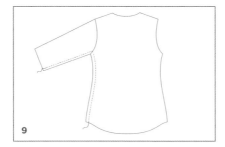

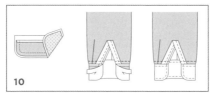

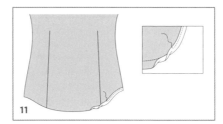

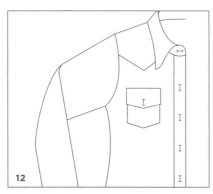

8. SLEEVE. Baste the cap of the sleeve within the seam allowance to help you ease the cap into the armhole. With the right sides together, pin the sleeve to the armhole edge, matching notches, and stitch. Pull the threads of the baste stitch (the bottom, bobbin thread) to gather up the cap a bit to ease into the armhole.

9. SIDE SEAMS. Stitch from hem to underarm and cuff to underarm. Finish the seams.

10. CUFFS. Fold back the top edge of the cuff (the one without interfacing), and with right sides together, stitch around the side and bottom edges. Turn the cuff and press. Pin the right side of the sleeve opening to the raw edge of the right side of the cuff. Stitch, and press the seam toward the cuff. Stitch the open edge to the sleeve. Topstitch around the entire cuff.

11. HEM. To make a baby hem, fold back the hem $1/4$", then again $1/4$". Topstitch all around the edge.

12. FINISHING. Mark the buttonholes on the right front of the shirt, the cuffs, and the pocket flaps. Sew the buttonholes. Sew the buttons on the opposite side to match where the buttonholes are.

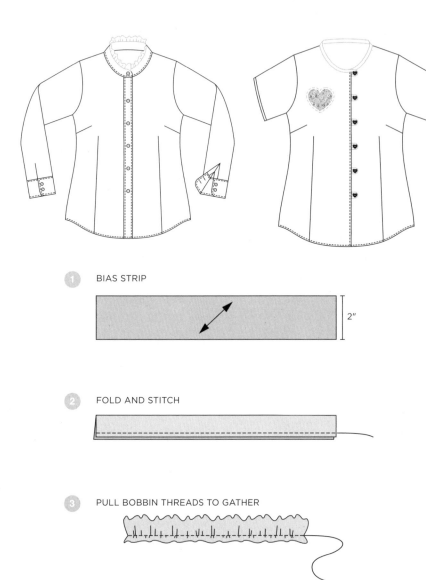

1 BIAS STRIP

2"

2 FOLD AND STITCH

3 PULL BOBBIN THREADS TO GATHER

The Collar

The basic shirt pattern included here has a pointed collar with a collar stand. This gives it a clean, classic, and polished look, but you can easily change it up. Some simple ideas:

REMOVE THE COLLAR

By sewing on the collar stand but not the collar itself, you can give a basic shirt a more feminine finish. Feel free to mix things up and cover the collar stand with a contrasting fabric. (To point out the obvious: If you remove the collar, there's no need for a button.) You can even remove the collar stand entirely and simply finish the neck opening with bias binding. Leave extra binding at the ends to turn back and stitch onto the back side to form a little loop-and-button closure. You might also try inserting a small ruffle inside the top edge of the collar stand. To do this, cut a 2"-wide strip of fabric, fold it in half, press, and use a basting stitch along the raw edges to gather. Sandwich the gathered edge of the ruffle between the collar stand pieces (right sides together) where the collar would normally be sewn. Stitch all three layers together. Turn the pieces right side out.

BUILT BY YOU
SHIRT DESIGN IDEAS

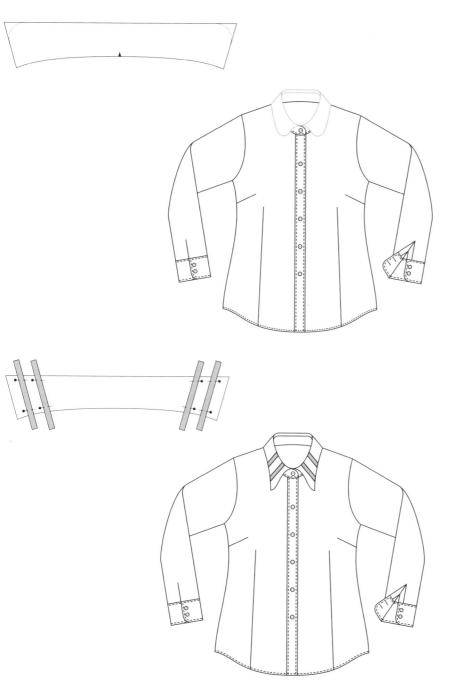

CHANGE THE COLLAR SHAPE

Instead of making a classic pointed-corner collar, you can cut the pattern piece differently to make a rounded corner. Or make the point more or less exaggerated. To do this, simply trace a new shape on the half, and cut it out.

ADD TRIM

The collar is a perfect place to get creative. Try pinning a piece of trim to the outside collar piece and top-stitching it on before you sew the collar pieces together. You can create a design with 1/4″ twill tape, top-stitching it on following the shape of the collar, or simply sew on pieces of lace, which will make a basic white cotton blouse all the more feminine.

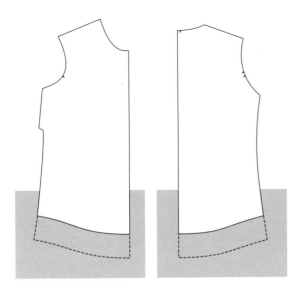

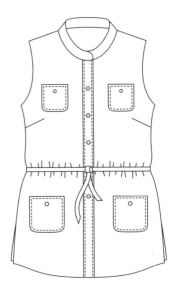

The Body

The basic pattern shape I've included will make an all-purpose, slim, flattering shirt. However, tweaking the fit can create an entirely different look. Why not try several versions?

LENGTH

To make a tunic-length shirt pattern from the basic shirt pattern, tape paper to the bottom of the front and back pattern pieces. Using your ruler, simply extend the lines of the side seams by about three to four inches. I recommend removing the darts (in other words, don't mark or sew them) so that you have a looser, longer look—a tight, long blouse probably won't look right, unless you're a pro basketball player. Loose tunics look great with a self-belt or pockets below the waist on the front of the shirt. This creates a beachy, casual look (I think it would be cute in a white eyelet cotton and worn with short denim shorts). You might want to add slits at the sides to allow for some

hip movement if the shirt hits hip level. To make slits, sew the side seams until a few inches before the hem (below the waist!), making sure that both slits start at the same premeasured point. Press the seams open and topstitch the seam allowance down for each slit.

HEM SHAPE

The basic pattern we'll be working with has a rounded dress-shirt hem, but you can also straighten it out or make it even curvier if you're so inclined. To do this, tape paper at the hem to the front and back pattern pieces, and trace a new shape. Generally speaking, it's a good idea to add side slits if the hem shape is straightened out.

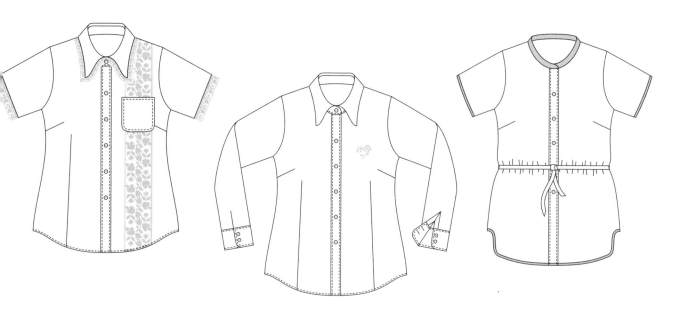

TRIMS, INSETS, AND APPLIQUÉS

Here's your chance to have fun! Make
your shirt out of some preppy oxford
fabric in the classic Ralph Lauren style,
but instead of that little horse emblem,
use a small iron-on appliqué to make
your own logo. Or buy some pretty
lace at a flea market and sew it down
the front of a delicate white cotton
batiste shirt. Sew the lace on using
a zigzag stitch and then, using small
scissors, cut out the fabric behind the
lace to create a lace inset. What about
finishing the hem with contrasting bias
binding instead of sewing a folded-
back hem? This looks especially good
if your hem shape is, well, shapely.

DECORATIVE STITCHING

You can add stitching anywhere on
your shirt, even if it's just for decoration. One technique I like is to add
rows of contrast stitching on the front
to create a mock yoke (more on those
in a minute). Experiment with different
shapes and thread colors.

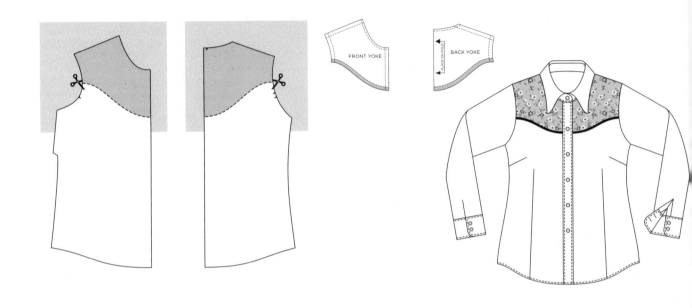

Adding Parts

Small details can make a huge difference in the look of a shirt. It's worth the extra effort to try a few new tricks every now and then!

YOKES

Yokes (for this chapter's purposes) are shaped pieces topstitched to the upper half of the shirt. The most obvious example is the classic western shirt, which has pointed yokes on the front and back. Yokes can take any shape you want and are a great opportunity to experiment: Try cutting them out of a contrasting fabric or inserting piping in the hems.

To make a yoke pattern piece, draw a design line in the shape of your yokes on your front and back pattern pieces. Lay a piece of paper underneath your pattern pieces and trace around the neck, shoulder, and armhole. Then, using your tracing wheel,

transfer that yoke design line to this new paper pattern. Use a pencil to fill in the dotted line made from your tracing wheel on your new pattern piece, then add a $1/2''$ seam allowance using your clear ruler. Cut out and you've got your yoke pattern.

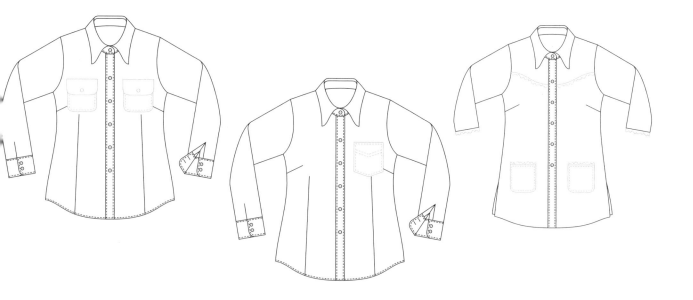

POCKETS

Once again, the array of options is almost mind-boggling. You can use one plain pointed pocket, like the one on a classic men's dress shirt, or use two with pocket flaps for a military-inspired look. You can have rounded or pointed pockets, contrast-fabric pockets, mini-pockets, pleated pockets, gathered pockets...I have included patterns for several shapes, but feel free to get creative and make your own. Pockets are a fun place to experiment with trims, buttons, and decorative stitching. And if you're having trouble deciding on a pocket shape, you can always prep your pockets and baste them onto the shirt. If they don't look right, pull them off with your seam ripper and try something else.

BELTS

You can easily make a belt out of your shirt fabric or, if you feel like it, contrasting fabric. Follow the instructions and use the pattern piece in the skirt chapter. Don't forget to attach a small belt loop to each side seam at the waist to hold your belt in place.

EPAULETS

Sewn onto a shirt's shoulders, these create a crisp, boyish, military-inspired effect. Or they can be attached to a short rolled sleeve to make a summer camp–style shirt. You can even double up the epaulets for design effect; to do this, simply trim the length of one of them.

To make an epaulet, cut two epaulet pattern pieces and sew along the seam allowances with the fabric face-to-face. Leave the end open, turn the epaulet inside out, and use your wooden point to push the points out. Press the epaulet and topstitch around the borders. Pin it to the shoulder atop the shoulder seam before joining the body to the sleeve. Tack the end of the epaulet with a button (no buttonhole needed). Try a decorative button, contrast fabric, or even striped trim on the epaulet. If you add trim, you must topstitch it to the face of the epaulet before sewing the epaulet pieces together.

 **1** SEW ALONG SEAM ALLOWANCES WITH PIECES RIGHT SIDES TOGETHER

 **2** TURN PIECE RIGHT SIDE OUT AND PRESS

 3 EDGE-STITCH

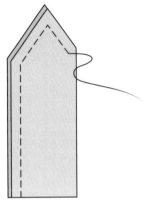

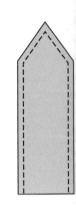

Front Facing

Front facing is used for finishing the area where you put your buttons and buttonholes. Some shirts don't have a separate front facing; they have folded-back front edges sewn the same way as a hem. Regardless, it's crucial to use interfacing because you need solid backing for the buttonholes. If it's too flimsy, the area around the buttonholes will sag and pucker.

TRIMS

You can insert any sort of piping or ruffle into the front facing seam. For a western look, try a piping and use the same piping on your yokes. Or, for a more feminine style, cut some strips of fabric on the bias, finish the edges, gather using a basting stitch to form ruffles, and sandwich them into your front facing.

SLIM FRONT FACING

You can change a shirt's look from sporty to sophisticated by slimming down the width of the facing. Simply skim off a little bit—how much is up to you. Just make sure you leave enough width for your button size.

145

TRY THIS!

You can play around with decorative or mismatched buttons, or even use inconsistent button spacing—who says you have to place your buttons evenly? Or make buttonholes for some of the buttons and then sew on other, nonfunctioning buttons for decoration.

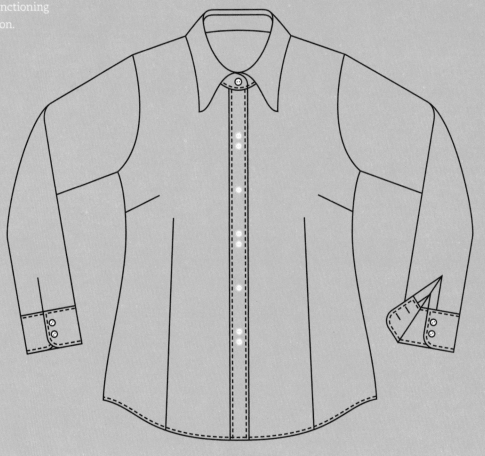

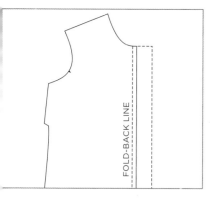

FOLD BACK ONTO FRONT

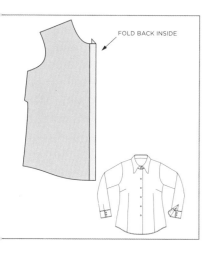

FOLD BACK INSIDE

MAKE A SELF-FACING

One of my favorite time-savers is to extend the front edge of the front pattern piece to make an all-in-one front; this will save you a little bit of sewing. To do this, tape a piece of paper to the front edge of the front pattern piece. Using your clear ruler, draw a parallel line about 2" from the old edge and cut along this line. The notch where you would have attached the front facing is now your folding point. When sewing, you can just finish the raw edge, fold it back, and edge-stitch. Don't forget to insert interfacing inside the fold!

The Sleeves

Sleeves don't have to be straight and narrow—they can take on almost countless shapes and styles. Here are some simple ways to change them up.

SHORTEN SLEEVES

Cut off the sleeve pattern at the desired length. (I suggest measuring a short-sleeved shirt you already have and like, and following that measurement.) Remember to add one inch for the sleeve hem. Or skip the hem and finish the raw edge with bias binding. One cute idea is to cut out a rounded shape in the center of the sleeve hem and

cover that raw edge with bias binding. Then leave a few extra inches of binding when you are finishing the bottom edge and use it to make a little bow.

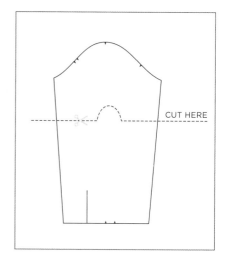

CUT HERE

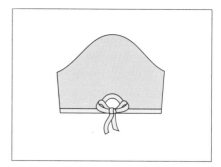

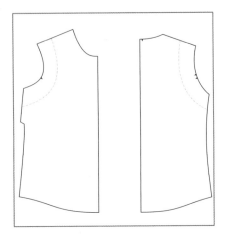

REMOVE SLEEVES

Sleeveless shirts are lifesavers in the summer. To make one, simply don't cut or sew the sleeve pieces.

To finish the edges of the body, the standard technique is to make facing: Trace the armholes of the front and back pieces, and make facing pieces about 2″ wide. To sew, stitch the facing pieces together and pin the right sides of the facing to the right side of the body. Stitch around the armhole, flip it over, under-stitch, and press the facing back. Then finish the edge of the facing. You can tack the facing to the side and shoulder seams inside.

Too complicated for you? A much easier way to finish a sleeveless shirt is to use bias binding to cover the raw edge. I don't recommend folding back the raw edge and sewing it like a hem, because the curve of the armhole will cause puckering (and be a tremendous pain to sew). If you want a cleaner look (in other words, no visible bias binding), make bias binding using the same fabric, sew it on, and then fold the binding back inside the armhole. Topstitch around to secure the binding inside.

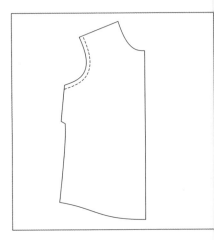

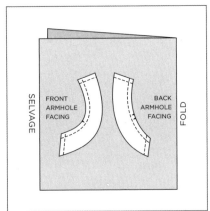

FRONT ARMHOLE FACING

BACK ARMHOLE FACING

SELVAGE

FOLD

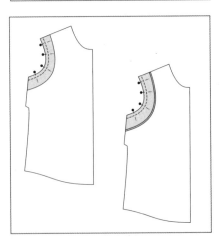

TRY THIS!

A sleeveless blouse can look cute with gathered shoulders. Here's how to make a summery gauze shirt with drawstrings.

1. Buy cotton cord and some beads or shells to tie on the ends.

2. Sew the side seams of the shirt, but not the shoulders yet!

3. Cover the armholes with bias binding.

4. Sew the shoulders together and press the seams open.

5. Topstitch down the pressed-open shoulder seams to create tunnels.

6. Insert the cords into the tunnels.

7. Finish the neckline. This stitching will anchor the cord into the neckline.

8. Pull the drawstrings to create gathered shoulders.

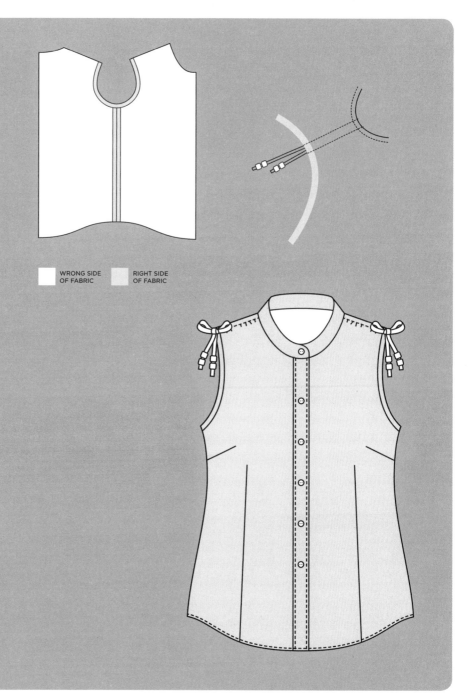

WRONG SIDE OF FABRIC

RIGHT SIDE OF FABRIC

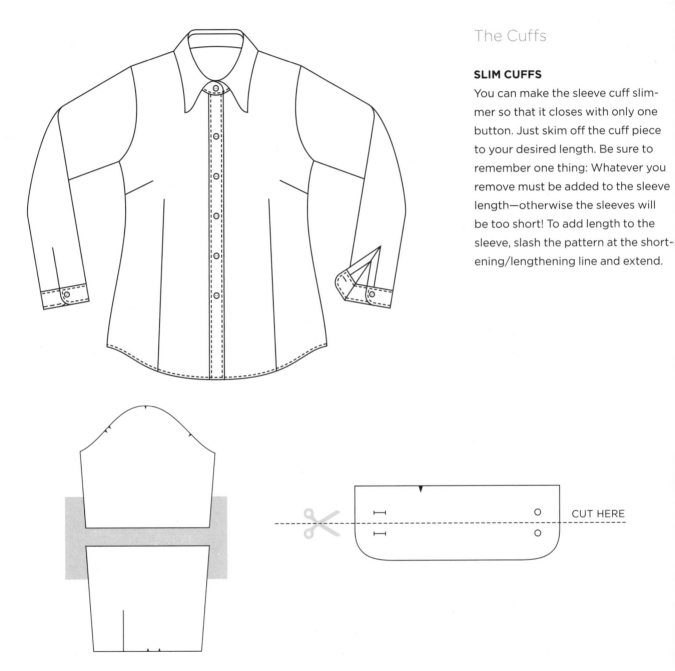

The Cuffs

SLIM CUFFS

You can make the sleeve cuff slimmer so that it closes with only one button. Just skim off the cuff piece to your desired length. Be sure to remember one thing: Whatever you remove must be added to the sleeve length—otherwise the sleeves will be too short! To add length to the sleeve, slash the pattern at the shortening/lengthening line and extend.

CUT HERE

REMOVE CUFFS

You can replace the cuffs with elastic to make gathered, puff-bottomed three-quarter-length sleeves. This looks especially good if you widen the sleeves.

Using your clear ruler, add 1″ to both side seams of each sleeve, starting from the top. Remove 2″ from the sleeve length. This new length includes the new hem seam allowance, which is 1″. Do not mark or sew a placket. To make the new sleeve, sew the sleeve hem and insert elastic inside. (Wrap the elastic around your forearm to figure out exactly how tight you want it to be.) Secure the elastic with stitching at each side seam. Sew the sleeve to the shirt body and then sew the side seams of the sleeve. There you go!

There you have it: The simple steps to make your very own shirt, with all the bells and whistles. I've come up with four varieties that look so different, you'd be shocked to think they all come from the same basic pattern. As with the skirt projects, I encourage you to get creative with buttons, trim, and details, and play with the patterns as you see fit. Use your project ticket to make sure you have everything in place before you get started, and proceed slowly and carefully—if you're sloppy, this is the garment where it will show the most!

BUILT BY YOU
PROJECTS

SHIRT PROJECT TICKET

STYLE:

TRIM NOTES:

PATTERN NOTES:

SEWING NOTES:

FABRIC AND TRIMS:

Project #1:
The Western Shirt

Banish thoughts of bucking broncos—
this cotton plaid shirt with solid-color
yokes, piping, and pearl snaps is perfect
paired with jeans for a low-key look.
If plaid is a bit too much for you,
make the shirt in summery gauze or
solid-color cotton.

SHIRT PROJECT TICKET

STYLE: WESTERN SHIRT

TRIM NOTES:
* 14-line white shirt button 1 for collar stand
* white cotton piping (1 yard)
* 11 pearl snaps — 2 on each cuff, 1 on each pocket flap, 5 down front — buy with snap fastener gun at sewing store

PATTERN NOTES:
* use angled pocket and flaps for front
* cut yokes in contrast fabric
* cut cuffs, front facing, pockets, and flaps on bias

SEWING NOTES:
* insert piping in front and back yokes, edge-stitch yokes down to body

FABRIC AND TRIMS:

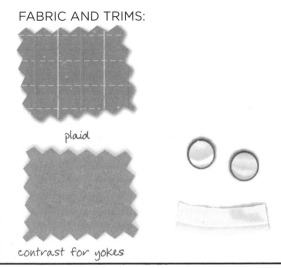

plaid

contrast for yokes

SHIRT PROJECT TICKET

STYLE: RUFFLE BLOUSE

TRIM NOTES:
* white fusible interfacing for front facing and collar stand (1/2 yard)
* 18-line 2-hole white shirt buttons for front (5)
* white 1/4" wide elastic (1/2 yard)

PATTERN NOTES:
* use only collar stand
* shorten sleeves
* add 1" to each side seam shortened sleeve to make wider for gathered look
* make front ruffle

SEWING NOTES:
* insert 8" of elastic into each sleeve
* insert ruffle into front facing

FABRIC AND TRIMS:

polka dot print

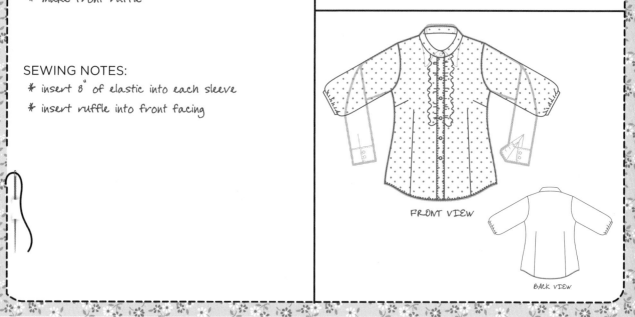

FRONT VIEW

BACK VIEW

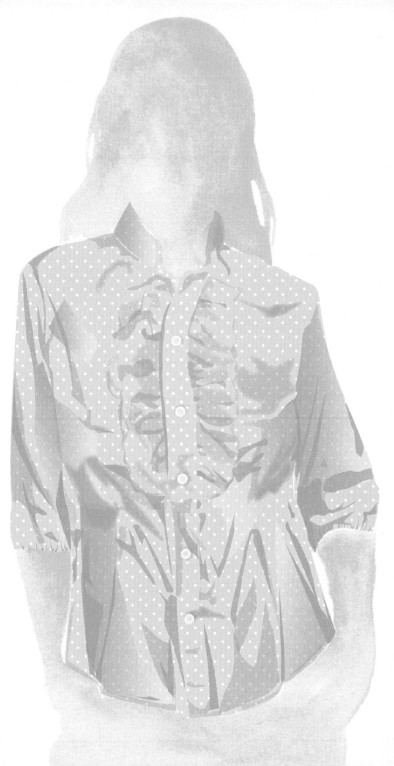

Project #2:
The Ruffle Blouse

Men may have pioneered the button-up shirt, but that doesn't mean yours has to be masculine. This one certainly isn't: It features a ruffle front, three-quarter-length elastic sleeves, and a mandarin collar. It's illustrated here in a yellow dotted swiss, but you could also make it in silk or silk chiffon for a dressier, winter-appropriate look.

Project #3: The Gauze Top

This shirt reminds me of the guay-abera, the classic summer men's shirt, but feminized. It's a white gauze tunic-length top, sleeveless, with beaded-drawstring shoulders, lace down the front, and lower patch pockets. The slim front facing is folded back, the hem is straight with side slits, and the fit is loose—only the bust darts are sewn.

SHIRT PROJECT TICKET

STYLE: GAUZE TOP

TRIM NOTES:
* 18-line 2-hole white shirt buttons for front; double-up buttons (8)
* white cotton cord (2 yards)
* white pony beads (12)
* white lightweight fusible for collar and stand only (1/4 yard)
* white cotton lace (2 yards)

PATTERN NOTES:
* change collar to rounded corners
* remove sleeves and cover armhole with bias binding in white cotton
* add to front edge to make folded back facing (no fusible needed)
* add 2" to front and back length
* add 4" side slits

SEWING NOTES:
* insert 2 strips of 18" of cord into each shoulder and tie on white pony beads to ends
* use very light fusible in collar and collar stand (white)
* topstitch 2 rows of cotton lace down left front and on pocket edges
* sew only bust darts on front — no darts sewn on back

FABRIC AND TRIMS:

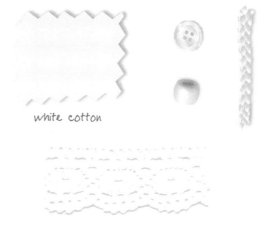

white cotton

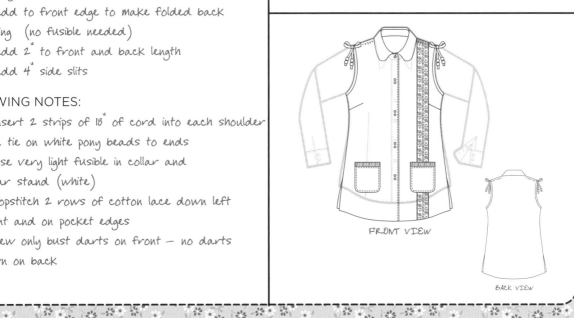

FRONT VIEW

BACK VIEW

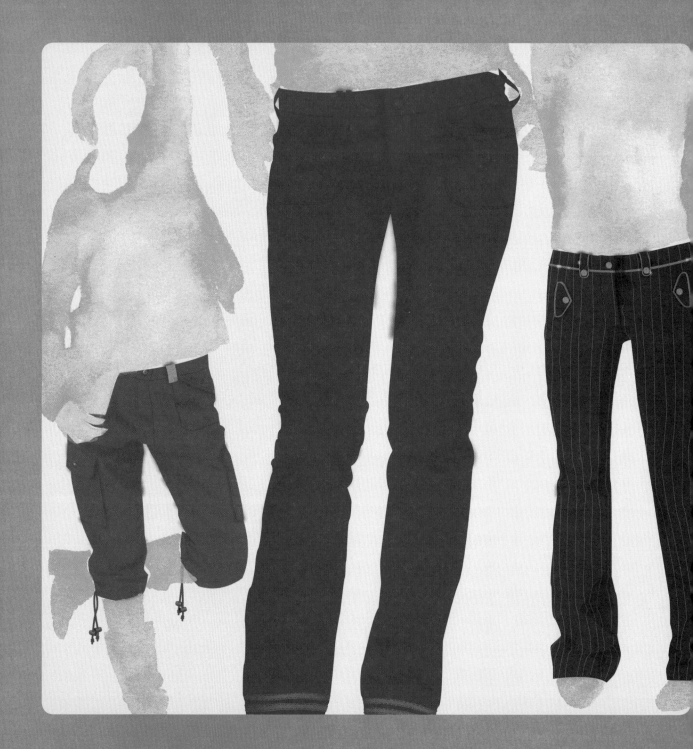

CHAPTER 8
PANTS

OVER THE YEARS, I'VE CHATTED UP QUITE A FEW OF MY CUSTOMERS, AND ONE THING THEY'VE ALL HAD IN COMMON IS A FIERCE DESIRE TO FIND A PERFECT-FITTING PAIR OF PANTS.

The pattern I've included—with a rise that's low-ish in a modern way but not too low, and a slight boot cut—is a staple of my collection and fits a large number of body types. in fact, I know a bunch of people who rarely wear anything else. I hope they look just as good on you!

The great thing about making your own pants is that once you've found the right pattern, you can create an entire wardrobe's worth of variations. (And this is almost certainly going to be the right pattern. As for the commercial pant patterns that have been available until now... well, let's just say things haven't changed much since Grandma's swinging-single days.) Sure, you can change colors and fabrics—charcoal-gray corduroy for winter, lightweight denim for spring—but the material is only the beginning. You can use decorative stitching and trim to make your pants your own. You can widen or narrow the legs. You can add different kinds of pockets, belt loops, and hardware. Whatever you decide to do, no one else will have a pair just like them—and that will make all your hard work worth it and then some.

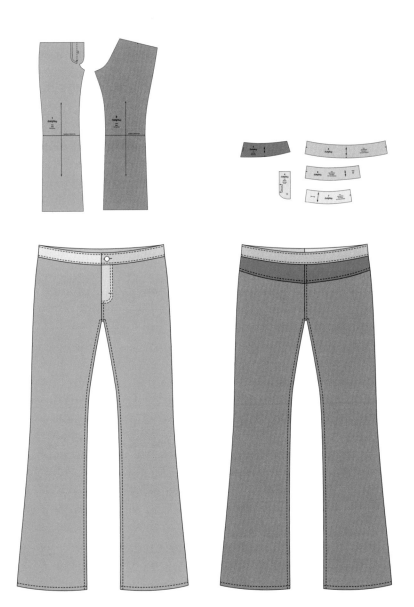

Project Specs

Difficulty Level: Advanced

Sewing Skills Needed: Joining seams, finishing seams, hemming, button attachment, buttonholes, edge stitching, topstitching, fly zipper insertion

PATTERN PIECES

Detail Pieces

I've also included several types of
detail pieces on the pattern sheets,
which you can use to add some
excitement to your basic pants. Let's
have a look at what they are and how
you can customize them.

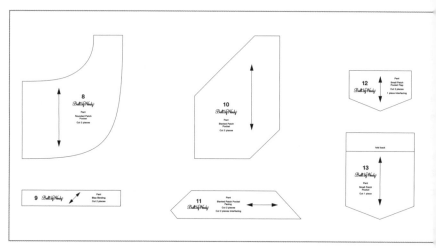

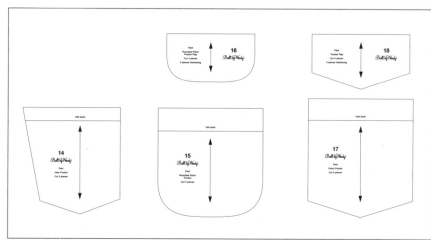

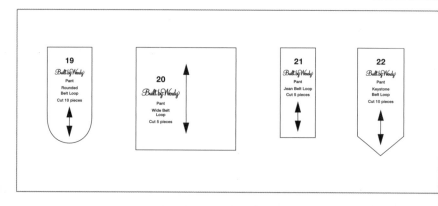

Here are a few suggested layouts that make the best use of your fabric. Note that these layouts cover the basic pant pattern but do not include the detail pieces. Buy at least an extra half yard to cut those from, depending on how many details your design includes and how much experimenting with pockets you plan on doing.

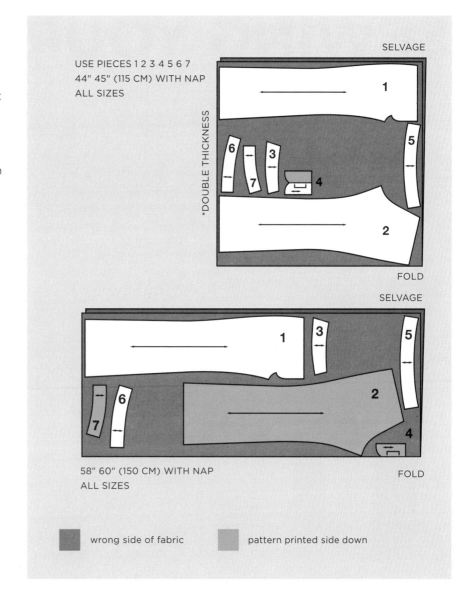

USE PIECES 1 2 3 4 5 6 7
44" 45" (115 CM) WITH NAP
ALL SIZES

SELVAGE

*DOUBLE THICKNESS

FOLD

SELVAGE

58" 60" (150 CM) WITH NAP
ALL SIZES

FOLD

wrong side of fabric   pattern printed side down

CUTTING

SEWING YOUR PANTS

Once your pant pieces are cut, you're ready to sew. Here are the steps to follow. If you've never made pants before, read through these first (and brace yourself—there's a lot to absorb).

1. FLY

A. Sew the front pieces right sides together along the front rise. Sew from the crotch to the circle marking, then baste from that point to the top edge.

B. Trim the right-side fly extension so that a $3/4''$ seam allowance remains. Make a clip on the front rise just below the fly extension. Finish the front rise and the left-fly edge with pinking, over-lock stitching, Seams Great, or a zigzag stitch.

C. Fold the right-fly piece, right sides together. Stitch the curved bottom and the side seam. Turn and press.

D. Stitch the zipper facedown on the right-fly trimmed seam allowance (*not* through the right-front pant).

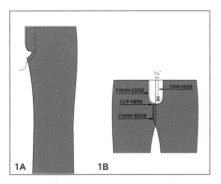

1A   1B

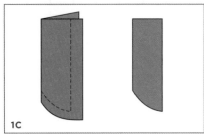

1C

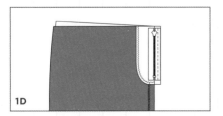

1D

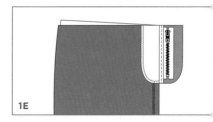

1E

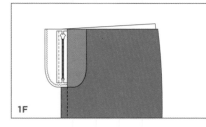

1F

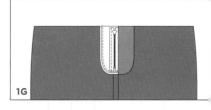

1G

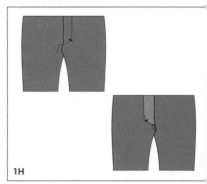

1H

E. Fold back the zipper, slide the right-fly piece underneath, and edge-stitch along the seam allowance, zipper, and right-fly piece.

F. Lay the other half of the zipper tape onto the left fly. While holding back the right fly, sew the zipper tape to the left fly only (not through the pant front body).

G. Topstitch down the left fly to the body, following the shape of the fly. You should still be holding back the right fly.

H. Turn the pants over and finish the fly topstitch line to the center front. Bar-tack the fly using a tight zigzag stitch—this secures the right fly to the body. Make the stitch line about ¼″ long.

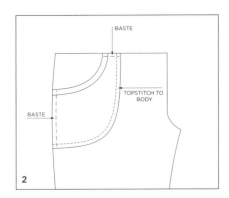

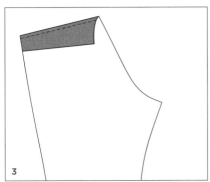

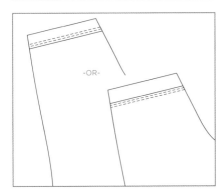

2. FRONT POCKETS. Pin the pocket to its position. Topstitch it down to the body. Baste the edges that end at the body's raw edge.

3. BACK YOKES. Stitch the back yoke to the back pieces (right sides together), finish this seam, press the seam allowance toward the back yoke side, and topstitch.

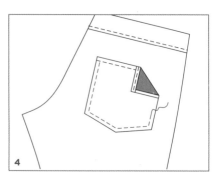

4

4. BACK POCKET. Topstitch to the body, measuring the position carefully.

5. CENTER BACK. With right sides together, stitch the center backs. I strongly recommend adding an extra row of stitching about $1/8''$ away from the seam on the lower curved part of the back seam for security. Anything you can do to prevent a hole ripping in this area will be more than worth the extra effort. Finish the seam, press it to one side, and topstitch the seam down.

6. LEG INSEAM AND OUTSEAM. With right sides together, stitch the front piece to the back piece at either the side seam or the inseam. This choice depends on which seam you are going to topstitch (if you choose to do that). For dressier pants, like those made of wool suiting, you probably wouldn't topstitch either seam. For corduroy or denim or any fabric or style that is more casual, top-stitch either the inseam or the outseam. It's up to you. I think that a topstitched outseam provides the most casual look. Whichever seam you decide to topstitch should be sewn first. Always sew from the hem up. Press the seam toward the pant front and topstitch if you'll be top-stitching. Sew the other leg seam (either the inseam or the outseam, whichever is left). Stitch an extra row when you get to the crotch area. Finish the seam and press. Repeat for the other leg.

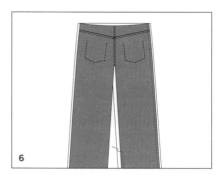

5

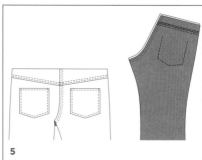

6

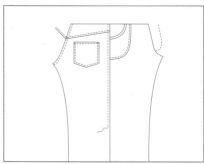

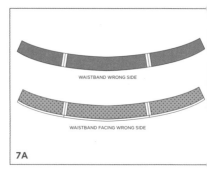

WAISTBAND WRONG SIDE

WAISTBAND FACING WRONG SIDE

7A

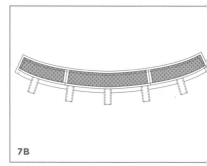

7B

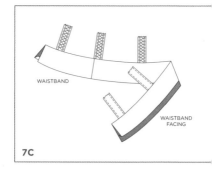

WAISTBAND

WAISTBAND FACING

7C

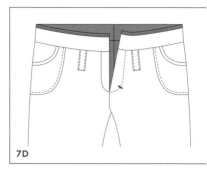

7D

7. WAISTBAND

A. Sew the waistband pieces together at the side seams. Apply interfacing to the waistband facing and fold back the bottom edge.

B. Pin the wrong side belt loops to the right side waistband's top edge. With the right sides together, stitch the waistband to the facing, sandwiching the belt loops into the waistband.

C. Turn the waistband right side out.

D. With right sides together, stitch the waistband to the body.

E. Tuck the seam allowance inside the waistband, turn up and press, and topstitch around the edges. Fold the belt loops down onto the body and bar-tack them down to the body.

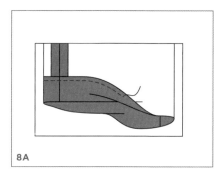

8A

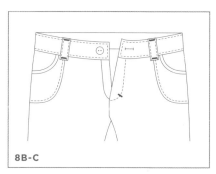

8B-C

8. FINISHING

A. Fold back the hem and topstitch.

B. Sew on the button and buttonhole.

C. Clip all loose threads and do a final pressing on all seams.

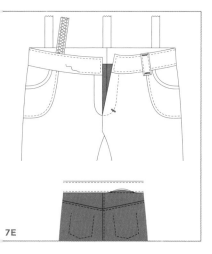

7E

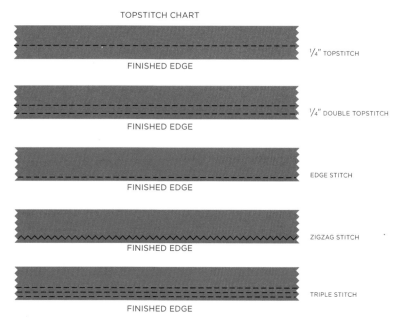

TOPSTITCH CHART

FINISHED EDGE — ¼" TOPSTITCH

FINISHED EDGE — ¼" DOUBLE TOPSTITCH

FINISHED EDGE — EDGE STITCH

FINISHED EDGE — ZIGZAG STITCH

FINISHED EDGE — TRIPLE STITCH

Pockets: Front

**THE ROUNDED FRONT
PATCH POCKET**

This pocket has an outer curved
edge, which you'll turn back and
press before topstitching it down to
the front piece of the garment. The
inner edge is covered with bias
binding; this is because it is difficult
to turn back without puckering
the pocket. The pockets' rounded
edges add a touch of femininity.

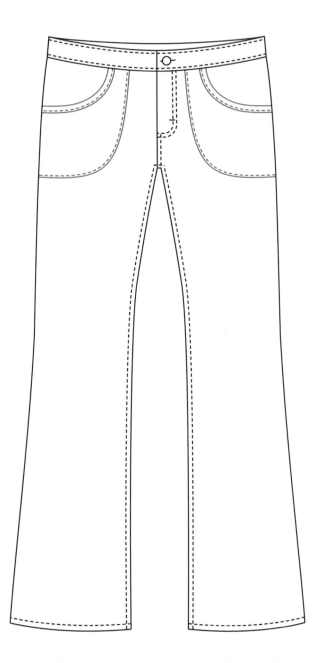

BUILT BY YOU
PANT DESIGN IDEAS

Bias binding

* Self-fabric binding: For a clean look, you can bind the opening of the pocket with the same fabric as the rest of your garment.

* Contrast binding: You might also try using a contrast color to liven up a plain pair of pants.

Piping

You can also insert piping along the outer edge of the pocket before top-stitching.

Contrast or decorative stitching

Try playing with the stitch type and positioning. Why not topstitch three rows instead of one and use three different-colored threads, one for each row? Or try a zigzag stitch instead of a straight one. You can even use thick embroidery thread and hand-stitch a loose running stitch or a messy zigzag for a rough, handmade look.

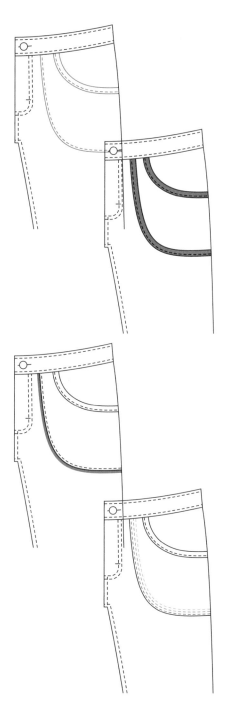

TRY THIS!

Different piping-and-fabric combinations create different looks. Two of my favorites:

Preppy: Leather piping on wool tweed pants.

Hippie: Natural jute piping with cotton canvas or denim pants.

TIP

Don't forget to stay-stitch rounded pockets! Otherwise, the outer curved edge will stretch out during sewing.

THE SLANTED FRONT PATCH POCKET

This pocket is angled, which gives it more of a unisex look. The outer edge is folded back, pressed, and topstitched to the garment. The inner edge (the pocket opening where you stick your hand in) has a facing. You could substitute bias binding here if you wanted, but the facing creates an opportunity to play with design.

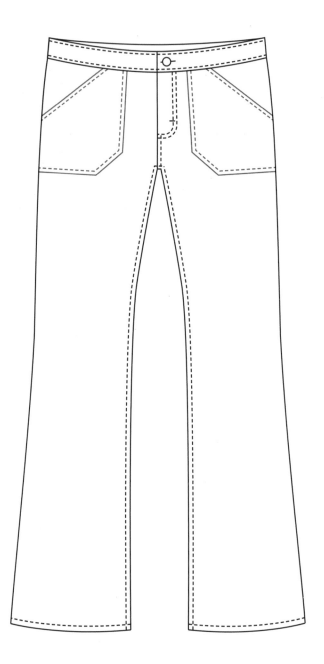

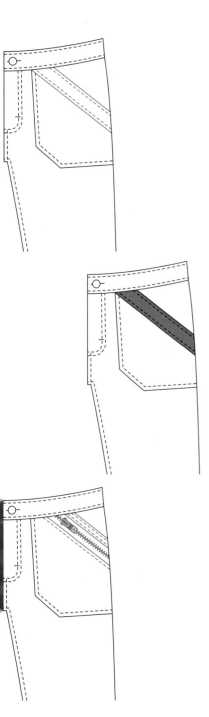

Pocket facing as detail

You can sew a facing on the outside of the pocket for decorative purposes, or on the inside, where you won't see it and it's simply functional. If you use it as a detail, you can use contrast topstitching or even cut the facing out of a contrast fabric. Remember all those old clothes you were going to throw away? Now is a good time to use them. Why not cut up an old shirt made out of a fabric you like and use it for facing?

Zipper

Inserting a zipper into the pocket opening is easy—just sandwich the zipper between the pocket and the facing. To do this, cover the raw edge of the zipper with a bias binding made out of the same fabric. Pin it to your garment. Topstitch the piece down around the outer edge and along the bias binding, and it will be secured to the body. Try adding a decorative zipper pull by tying a piece of cord or fabric through the eye of the zipper.

With hardware

Try adding a D-ring for clipping your keys—it's functional and adds a touch of toughness. (When topstitching the outer edge of the pocket, you can insert anything inside the seam.) Make a fabric loop about an inch long and slide the D-ring through it; then slip the ends of the loop under the pocket's outer edge seam. The loop will be secured to the body of the pants while you are topstitching the pocket down. For more reinforcement, topstitch back and forth a few times.

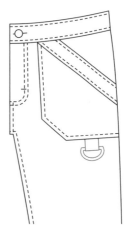

THE SMALL PATCH POCKET WITH FLAP

This is a small pocket that is very versatile (you can move it around, since it's not secured at the side seams).

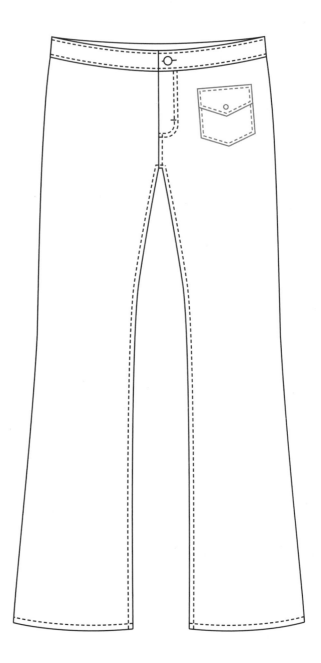

DOUBLE POCKETS

Place pockets on both front pieces or remove the flaps for simple patch pockets. You might try adding a button near the top of each for detail.

FLAPS ONLY

You can create a mock pocket using only the flaps. Play with the positioning to make it flattering. Or, if you feel like it, double them up on one side only.

 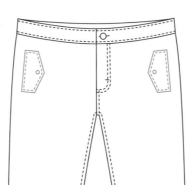 

Pockets: Back

THE JEAN-STYLE BACK POCKET

This is the classic patch pocket shape. Because jean-style pants fit snugly, the backs of them should always have patch pockets as opposed to welt pockets (the kind that go inside the garment). This type of pocket can be made bigger or smaller or positioned differently to really flatter your backside. Before you commit, you might want to make several varieties, pin them on, and try each one in front of a three-way mirror (or a brutally honest friend).

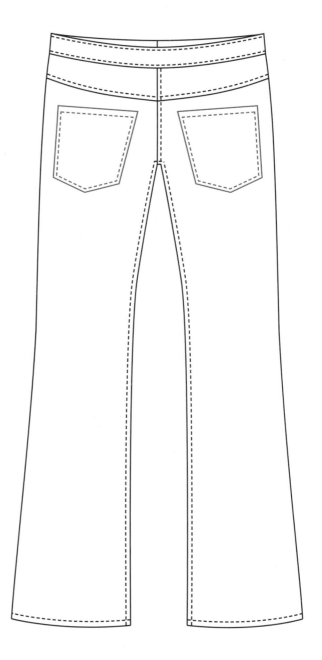

Decorative stitching

There are more jean companies out there than anyone can keep track of, and the way they distinguish themselves is through decorative pocket stitching. The stitching signals the brand, so why not make your own brand? Try different colors or shapes, or use thick embroidery thread and sew your design by hand.

Cutouts

You can make a cutout shape anywhere on your garment, but I like it best on the back pockets. All you need to do is make a facing.

Here's how:

1. PIN A SCRAP OF FABRIC (I would use the same fabric or something in a similar color) to the pocket face-to-face so that the front of the facing and the front of the pocket are "kissing."

2. TRACE A SHAPE that you want to cut out on the wrong side of the facing. Use your chalk pencil or even just a marker. (No one is going to see these markings; they will be hidden inside.)

3. STITCH ALONG your drawing line.

4. CUT OUT THE CENTER of the shape about 1/4" away from the stitch line.

5. PULL THE FACING through the hole to the other side. Use your fingers to straighten it all out.

6. PRESS and topstitch around the hole.

Appliqués

You can make an appliqué out of anything. To add stability to home-made appliqués, I recommend buying this stuff called Stitch Witchery. It's a double-sided adhesive fabric—just like fusible interfacing, except that it fuses on both sides. Take a scrap of fabric and iron this onto the back. Then cut out your appliqué shape, iron it onto your pocket, and use a tight zigzag stitch around the raw edge to finish the appliqué. For a nice appliqué stitch, I recommend setting your stitch length to 0.5 or less, and your width to 2.5. You can make it less wide, but be sure to cover the edge of the appliqué. Use a silky thread, something with sheen. The company Sulky makes a large assortment of colored embroidery threads that have a certain shine to them. Try making an appliqué using a few fabrics of varying prints, textures, and colors.

POCKET POSITIONING

This is the most essential element in creating pants that flatter your backside. Before sewing the back pockets on—or adding elaborate appliqués, decorative stitching, or cutouts—you might want to play with different positions by basting or pinning pockets on. (Now is the time to call up that brutally honest friend of yours.) You can:

Move the pockets up or down.

Move the pockets horizontally. The farther apart they are, the wider your butt looks. This can be a good or a bad thing. No matter what, though, don't place them too close together because that just looks weird.

Play with angles. Tilting the pockets outward creates a more rounded look, which is good if you have no butt.

Make the pockets smaller. Just trim around the seam allowance. Don't go overboard—anything in the ¼"-to-½" range makes a big difference.

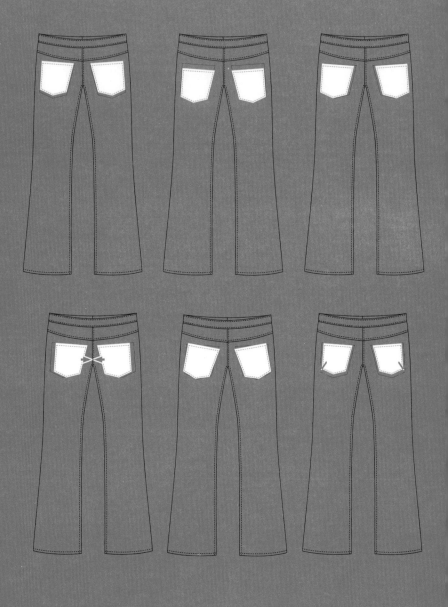

THE BACK PATCH POCKET
WITH FLAP

This is a great basic back pocket. It can look utilitarian on army-style pants or it can give dressier pants a carefree twist.

Design-wise, it makes the most sense to pair angular pockets with other angular details, as opposed to mixing rounded and angular details. For instance, if your front pockets are angular and not rounded, you might want to use the angled keystone belt loops (we'll get to those soon) and this back pocket.

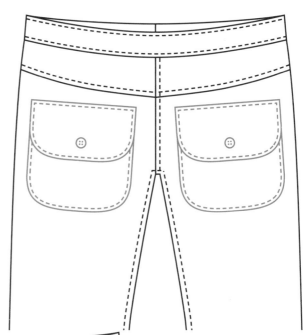

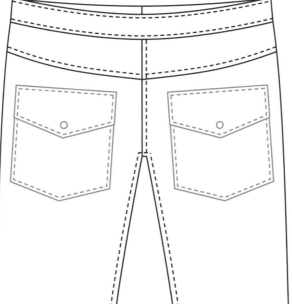

Double button

You can place one center button on the pocket flap or you can try two, with one placed in each corner. This looks nice with diagonal buttonholes. Don't forget to measure carefully to make sure the buttons are in the same places on each pocket!

Trim tape

You can topstitch any sort of trim tape horizontally or vertically across the pocket or the flap. For extra detail, team up two or three colors, or use striped trim.

Contrast pocket flap

Try using the reverse side of the fabric, or another fabric entirely, for the pocket flap. I like to do this with this pocket style when I'm working with denim. The contrast breaks up the back view, creating a flattering look.

Contrast pocket flap lining

Try using a bright contrasting color, or even a cute print, to line the pocket flap. It also looks nice if you use contrast stitching on the garment to match the lining. Look through your scraps to find something.

Mock-welt pocket flap

Welt pockets are pretty advanced, and I don't get into them in this book, but you can get a similar look by simply stitching on the flaps alone. This is a great trick when you're working with men's suiting fabric.

Belt Loops

THE CLASSIC BELT LOOP

This is the most common belt loop shape. Since it is so basic, it's fun to play around with customization.

Placement

Try changing up the location of belt loops on pants: You can use seven loops instead of the classic five or even try double loops placed half an inch apart.

Crisscross

Try crisscrossing the center back loop for a work wear–inspired feel; this is a great trick if you're making, say, white painter's pants. Just be sure to make the loops you'll be crossing longer.

Contrasting color

Why not change the color or fabric of the belt loops? Try a pair of denim pants with red belt loops on the front; you can even make leather ones (use a leather needle) for a tough-yet-luxe look.

Length or width

I've included a wide belt loop pattern piece, which looks slightly more unexpected than the standard pattern but allows for the same experimentation with detail. You can also add or subtract from the length of your belt loops, which is an important change to make if you prefer wearing very wide or very narrow belts.

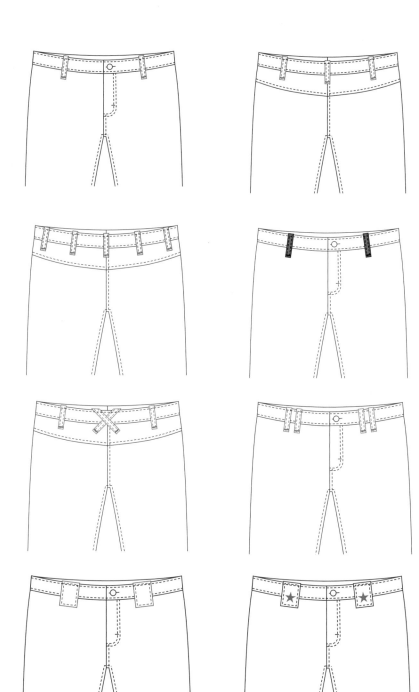

THE ROUNDED BELT LOOP

This nontraditional shape is the perfect finish for pants with rounded pockets. It's also a simple way to add a little something extra to a basic pair of pants.

Tack with buttons

Try securing the belt loops with buttons instead of the usual bar-tack stitch. Use a colorful or decorative button for added detail and contrast.

Decorative tack

Instead of the usual horizontal bar-tack stitch at the bottom of the belt loop, try a crisscross. You can also make a matching X bar tack on the fly to match. Try forming the X out of two colors or using thick embroidery thread to emphasize it even more.

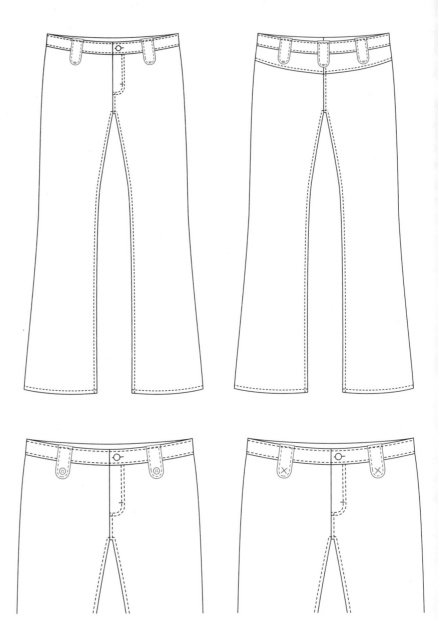

THE KEYSTONE BELT LOOP

This angled belt loop can look western or military, or both.

Tape trim

Topstitch a piece of decorative tape (how about stripes?) vertically down the length of the loop. Be sure to do this before sewing the belt loop together.

Piped edge

You can insert piping into the seam of the belt loop in the same way you would do anywhere else. Try matching the piping to the buttons on the pockets.

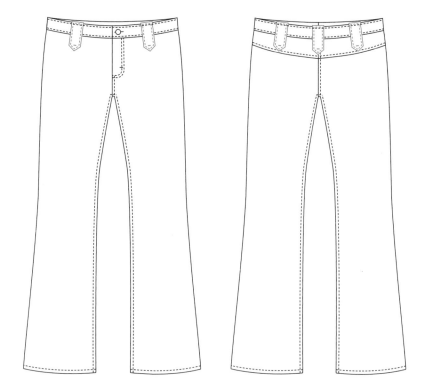

Pattern Changes

Another way to change your basic
pants is to alter the width of the
legs. This is a pretty easy way to customize the fit. The process of tweaking
other fit details is a bit advanced for
a novice, so I don't get into it in this
book, but working with the leg is a
good way to get comfortable with
some pattern-making.

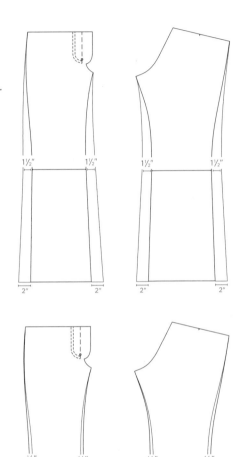

WIDENING THE LEGS

Start by taping paper along the front
and back leg pattern pieces, on both the
inseam and the outseam. Make marks
at the knee notches and bottom openings indicating the width you want to
add. Remember, when working on the
seams of a pant leg, that you must work
in quarters: There's a back and a front,
and two sides for each. So, for instance,
if you want to make the bottom opening 8″ bigger, you'll add 2″ to the front
inseam, front outseam, back inseam,
and back outseam. Four seams with 2″
added to each equals 8″ total added.
Once you've decided what to add at
the bottom opening and knee, use your
ruler to blend the line from the hem up
to the crotch. This is your new pattern!

NARROWING THE LEGS

This works the same way as widening
the legs, but you make marks inside the
pattern instead of outside. If you want
to make fairly narrow legs, remove $1/2$″
at each knee seam (making the knee 2″
smaller) and $3/4$″ at the bottom opening
(removing 3″ total). If you remove more
than that, you might need to insert a
zipper or slit in the side seam at the
bottom so that you can fit your foot
through the opening. You can also sew
your pants and then skim in the leg
when you're done, pinning beforehand
to get a precise fit. Just blend any nar-
rowing up from the knee to the crotch.

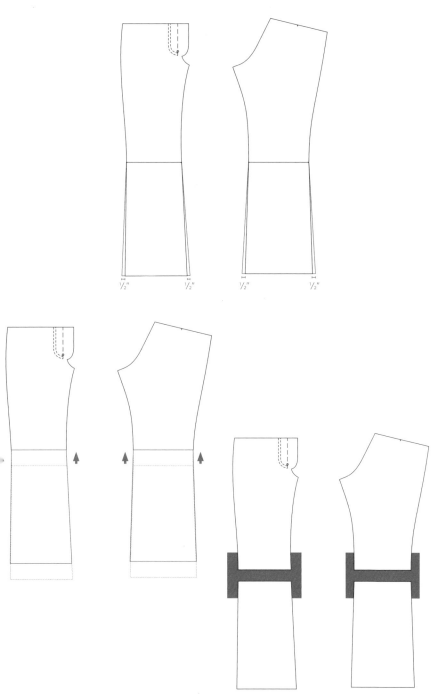

BOOT CUT

If you want your pants to have a more exaggerated boot cut, remaining slim in the thigh, keep the knee the same, add to the bottom opening, and connect the points. A popular guideline for boot-cut pants is to add $1/2''$ to each bottom opening seam so that the new bottom opening is 2" bigger.

SHORTENING AND LENGTHENING

There are a few ways to lengthen or shorten pants. Usually, you either fold or extend at the shortening/lengthening line on the pattern to preserve the overall shape of the pant leg. You could also just add or subtract a bit of length from the bottom opening. However, because the pants here flare slightly, they will become more flared if you add length at the bottom and less flared if you subtract it. Also, don't forget to take your hem allowance into account!

Here are some project ideas that utilize many of the techniques discussed so far. However, as you've probably realized by now, you already have the tools to do whatever you want. Feel free to mix up the possibilities—your project ticket will help you figure out what you want to do and what you need to do it.

BUILT BY YOU
PROJECTS

PANT PROJECT TICKET

STYLE:

TRIM NOTES:

FABRIC AND TRIMS:

PATTERN NOTES:

SEWING NOTES:

Project #1:
The Army Capris

You can't go wrong with this casual classic. For spring, as illustrated, you can make them Capri-length and use a lightweight cotton twill or canvas. For fall, why not make them full-length out of wool tweed and trim them with leather buttons? These pants have slanted front patch pockets with zippers and knotted-cord zipper pulls, round back patch pockets with contrast flap linings and double buttons, round patch pockets on the sides, drawstring bottom openings with cords inserted in the hems, and wide belt loops with contrast tape that matches the contrast flap linings.

PANT PROJECT TICKET

STYLE: ARMY CAPRIS

TRIM NOTES:
* 7" regular olive zip (3 – 2 for pockets & 1 for fly)
* 1/4"-wide orange cotton tape (3/4 yard)
* 32-line army-colored 2-hole buttons (7 – 2 on each back flap, one on each side flap, one on waistband)
* army-color cotton cord for hem drawstring (2 yards – 1 yard for each leg)
* drawstring stays (4 pieces – 1 for each string)
* orange cotton twill for pocket flap facing (1 yard)
* black fusible interfacing for pocket flaps and waistband (1 yard)

PATTERN NOTES:
* use slanted front patch pockets
* use round back patch pockets on back & sides
* use wide belt loops (5 of them)
* shorten pants to Capri length
* cut bias binding for front pocket zip edge

SEWING NOTES:
* insert zip in slanted front patch pockets cover edge with self-fabric bias binding
* topstitch tape on belt loops
* insert cotton cord into hem for drawstring
* double topstitch around side and back pockets/ flaps, front slanted pockets, fly, and inseam
* cut all pieces in self (army green canvas) except pocket flaps and waistband facing in contrast fabric (orange)

FABRIC AND TRIMS:

olive green cotton canvas

contrast fabric

tape for belt loops

cord for hem drawstring

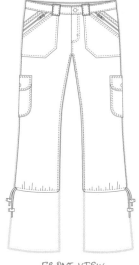
FRONT VIEW

BACK VIEW

PANT PROJECT TICKET

STYLE: SAILOR PANTS

TRIM NOTES:
* 7" regular navy zipper
* metallic gold piping (1 yard)
* 32-line gold anchor buttons (10 buttons — 1 on each back flap, 1 on each front flap, 1 on waistband, 1 on each belt loop)
* black fusible interfacing for pocket flaps and waistband (1 yard)

PATTERN NOTES:
* use pant pocket flaps on back
* use small front patch pocket flaps on front
* use rounded belt loops (5)
* add to front and back legs to make wide leg

SEWING NOTES:
* insert piping into waistband, belt loops, and in all pocket flaps
* secure belt loops with gold buttons

FABRIC AND TRIMS:

navy stripe tropical wool suiting

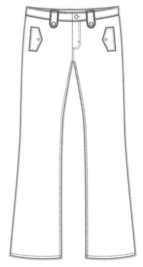

FRONT VIEW   BACK VIEW

Project #2:
The Sailor Pants

This is a wide-leg pant with piping and gold buttons. It uses angled front and back mock-pocket flaps, and has button-tacked rounded belt loops. Experiment with a variety of fabrics and colors: For fall, you might want to use lightweight navy wool suiting (maybe even a pinstripe); for spring, go for a gray cotton cavalry will (this type of fabric has exaggerated twill lines) with white piping.

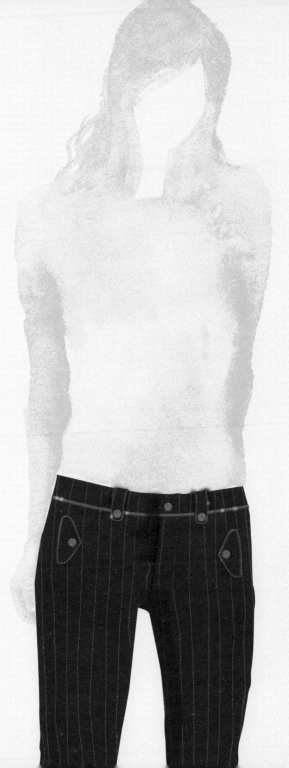

Project #3: The Skinny Cords

With slim legs and front patch pockets, this pair is sleekly feminine yet low-key. You could shorten the pattern to make girlish Capri pants or keep the pants long to scrunch at the ankle over heels or stuff into a pair of boots. I've added double belt loops and trim along the hem to spice up the simple style. In corduroy, as shown, it's a perfect fall piece, but it would be equally useful in twill or stretch denim. Why not make them all?

PANT PROJECT TICKET

STYLE: SKINNY CORDS

TRIM NOTES:
* 7" regular brown zipper
* brown leather 1/4"-wide trim (1 yard)
* 32-line brown leather shank button (1)
* black fusible interfacing for waistband (1/4 yard)

FABRIC AND TRIMS:

brown cord

PATTERN NOTES:
* slim front and back legs from knee down to hem — remove 3/4" off each seam at hem and blend up knee
* add rounded front patch pockets
* cut 7 belt loops (3 on back and 4 on front)

SEWING NOTES:
* topstitch trim around hem
* double up on front belt loops
* cover front pocket edge with self-fabric bias binding

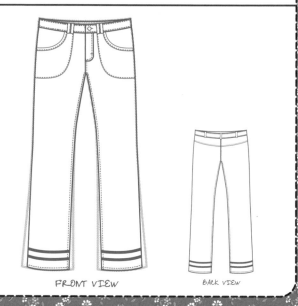

FRONT VIEW   BACK VIEW

CHAPTER 9

PLAN B

Take It to Your Tailor

TOTALLY OVERWHELMED? I'LL BE THE FIRST TO ADMIT THAT SEWING REQUIRES LOADS OF TIME AND PATIENCE—AND QUITE A FEW PEOPLE HAVE NEITHER TO SPARE.

Still, don't despair. There's a way to experience the thrill of the design process and leave the dirty work to someone else—someone who knows exactly what he or she is doing. Meet your new best friend: the neighborhood tailor.

You might not have realized this, but tailors can do a lot more than hem pants and fix loose buttons. They're trained in the art of sewing, and if you hand them a pattern, they can make it. Professionally. It will cost you, but you'll still end up paying less than you would for a designer version of the same piece.

What this leaves you to do is:

1. BUY FABRIC. Consult the yardage guide in chapter 2. If you can afford it, I strongly encourage you to buy a couple of extra yards for insurance. Not that you should *expect* the tailor to make a mistake, but, hey, you never know. After all, if you were sewing the design yourself, you'd probably botch something—isn't that why you're handing it over to someone else? Friends of mine have gone to some of the priciest tailors in Manhattan and come out with something other than what they expected. Be prepared for that possibility, and you'll ultimately be happy with the results. (And you can always make something else with the leftovers.) As you would with a garment you'd make yourself, you must preshrink—wash and dry the fabric several times if that's how you'll care for it, or dry-clean it.

2. BUY NOTIONS AND TRIMS. You'll need interfacing—the tailor might have some in the shop, but it's better to buy the best type for your fabric. Assemble buttons, zippers, and anything else you might need in a plastic zip-closure bag. Here's your chance to get creative: Do you want to add lace trim or piping? Do you want to use brightly colored contrast thread for topstitching? Do you want Great-grandma's crocheted drink coaster to be sewn on as an appliqué? If you're interested in upgrading to something you're not advanced enough to sew yourself—an invisible zipper, say—go for it. A tailor will know how to handle it.

3. CAREFULLY FILL OUT A PROJECT CARD for your design. This will give the tailor a clear, logical blueprint for what you want and how you want it. Draw your design very carefully—clearly indicate the style, fit, trim, and stitching. If you're not a budding Picasso, here's a hint: Buy some tracing paper. You can then go over the outlines of the designs in this book to get the shape and proportions right.

4. MEASURE YOURSELF. Determine the size you'll need in the garment you're having made according to the guidelines in chapter 3. You can carefully cut out your size on the pattern or play it safe and have the tailor handle this. Just don't forget to bring the pattern with you!

5. MAKE SURE YOU INCLUDE EXTRA PATTERN PIECES you'll need from this book, such as custom pockets, sleeves, and collars.

SIZE WISE

You might want to have your tailor leave the hems of pants and skirts unfinished. That way, you can try on the almost-finished garment and have him or her measure the precise point where *you* want the hem to fall. The hemming can probably be done while you wait. But even if it takes an extra day or two, you'll save yourself the risk of not getting exactly what you want. (Remember, pants that have already been hemmed can only be taken out so far.)

If you're tall or tiny, or have other figure issues that will affect the fit of a basic pattern, talk things over with your tailor. My patterns come with lines for lengthening or shortening, and a good tailor will be able to accommodate just about any request. For instance, if you're 6' 3" and have trouble finding pants that don't fit like floods, let the tailor know and have him or her extend the pattern to allow for your long legs.

SEEING DOUBLE: THE COPYING OPTION

You may not have realized it, but a good tailor can also copy just about anything. This can open up a whole new world. If you've found fashion's holy grail—a perfect-fitting pair of pants—why not have a duplicate pair made in denim and another in corduroy with different pockets and contrast topstitching? You can also give a tailor a few garments and have him or her re-create different elements from each of them to make a new item—using the collar and pockets from one shirt, the sleeves of another, and the body of a third to make the shirt of your dreams, for example. If you can envision it, it can happen. Fill out a project card—or at least draw a sketch—to make sure that you and the tailor are (literally) on the same page.

GLOSSARY

BACKSTITCH A few machine stitches in reverse, sewn at the beginning and end of a seam to secure the threads. Most machines have a button to activate this automatically, or you can do it by hand by turning your hand wheel away from you.

BAR TACK A back-and-forth stitch used to attach a belt loop or secure a perpendicular line of stitching.

BASTING STITCH A long stitch used not to join seams permanently but to secure fabric in preparation for joining. This stitching is often removed after sewing, but not always.

BIAS The imaginary line at a 45-degree angle to the lengthwise and crosswise grains of woven fabric. This is where fabric stretches the most.

BIAS BINDING Also known as bias tape. A thin strip of fabric cut on the bias, used to envelop the raw edge of a hem or seam. It can be bought prepackaged or made from your own fabric and scraps. A bias tape maker helps speed the process.

BLIND HEM A hem that is virtually invisible from the outside of a garment because the thread only pricks the surface occasionally. A special foot is required to accomplish this using a machine. Not recommended for beginners.

BLOCKING The process of straightening fabric before sewing by pulling it so that lengthwise and crosswise grains meet at a 90-degree angle.

BOBBIN A tiny spool inserted inside the sewing machine, usually underneath the needle hole. The bobbin thread links with the needle thread to form each stitch.

CROSSWISE GRAIN The direction of fabric weave that runs from selvage to selvage, or horizontally. Also known as the weft.

DART A wedge-shaped marking on a pattern that is sewn into a tuck to give shape to a garment to better fit the contours of the body.

EASE The process of spreading out the difference in length when joining a longer section of fabric to a shorter one, so as to avoid bunching and leftover fabric in a seam.

EDGE STITCH A line of stitching run extremely close to a folded edge or a seam line. Produces a neater,

dressier look and is usually sewn with a shorter stitch length.

FACING Fabric pieces that are mirror images of pattern pieces. Commonly used to finish openings such as necklines, front shirt openings, and armholes. Linings are also facings.

GRAINLINE Generally speaking, this refers to the lengthwise grain on a piece of fabric—the direction of the weave that runs parallel to the selvage and is the strongest direction of the weave.

GRAINLINE ARROWS These mark the direction of the grainline on patterns to indicate where on the fabric in relation to the grainline the pattern pieces should be placed.

HEM A common method of finishing a raw edge by turning it under twice and stitching. Also refers to the bottom edge of a garment.

INTERFACING A special layer of fabric, not visible from the outside of a garment, joined to the back of fabric to support delicate and detailed areas such as collars, cuffs, and pockets. Comes in sew-on and fusible varieties; fusible interfacing is simply ironed to the back of the fabric.

LENGTHWISE GRAIN The direction of fabric weave that runs parallel to the selvage, or vertically, and is the strongest direction of the weave. Also known as the warp.

MITERING The process of perfectly matching up stripes or plaids when two pieces of fabric cut on the bias meet at a seam.

MUSLIN Usually made of cotton, this is an inexpensive fabric used to make test garments before sewing with more expensive material.

NAP The raised surface of a fabric that changes appearance when brushed or viewed from different angles. Napped fabrics, unlike regular fabrics, must always be cut in the same direction.

NOTIONS Everything you use to sew that isn't fabric or trim—needles, thread, interfacing, buttons, zippers, and the like. It's best to stock up on notions so you won't need to run out and buy something every time you start a new project.

ONE-WAY FABRICS Fabrics that have a nap or a special print, and thus must be cut in one direction only.

PINKING Finishing an edge with pinking shears, which produces a zigzag cut and prevents many fabrics from fraying. This is the easiest way to finish a seam.

PLACKET An opening or slit in a garment. In this book, it refers to the opening above a sleeve's cuff, which is finished with bias binding.

PRESSER FOOT The changeable device on a sewing machine that holds the fabric in place during sewing. Special presser feet are required for specific tasks such as sewing a zipper.

RIGHT SIDE/WRONG SIDE The right side of a fabric is the side designed to be seen. The wrong side is the "back." However, you may choose to use the wrong side as a design accent or even make a garment with the wrong side out. If so, designate it the "right" side for the purposes of the instructions in this book. Pieces are often sewn "face-to-face," which means right side to right side.

ROTARY CUTTER AND MAT A wheel-shaped blade used to cut fabric pieces quickly and efficiently with less strain on the wrist. It must be used with a self-healing mat to prevent damage to the surface beneath.

SEAM A line of stitching that joins two pieces of fabric.

SEAM ALLOWANCE The area between the edge of the cut fabric piece and the line where the seam goes. In this book, it is $1/2''$ for most areas and $1/4''$ for small areas such as necklines. Seam allowances are built into the patterns in this book, but if you alter the shape of a pattern, you must take the seam allowance into account.

SEAM RIPPER A small tool used to tear open seams without cutting into fabric.

SELVAGE The finished side edges of a bolt of fabric.

SERGER A type of sewing machine that uses multiple spools of thread to sew, trim, and finish seams simultaneously. Used to make professional-quality knits. Not for beginners.

SHANK The stem of a button.

STAY STITCH A basting stitch applied along the seam allowance. This is done to a piece before joining it to another piece to stabilize delicate areas and prevent stretching.

THREAD TENSION The balance between the needle and the bobbin threads in a machine stitch. If one of the threads pulls with more tension than the other, the stitch will not meet in the center of the fabric. Must be calibrated before sewing a garment.

THROAT PLATE The metal plate surrounding the needle hole on a sewing machine, marked with lines indicating varying seam-allowance widths.

TOPSTITCH A stitch sewn on the right side of a garment about $1/4''$ from a finished edge. Can be functional or decorative.

UNDER STITCH When a seam allowance is folded over and hidden inside facing, this stitch joins the seam allowance to the facing. The wrong side of the fabric faces up during sewing.

WARP Also known as the lengthwise grain or grainline of a fabric. Runs parallel to the selvage and is the strongest direction of the fabric.

WEFT Also known as the crosswise grain of a fabric. Runs from selvage to selvage.

YOKE A shaped panel of fabric that is topstitched onto or inserted into a garment for decorative or shaping purposes.

ZIGZAG STITCH A Z-shaped machine stitch that allows for more stretch and is thus used for knits. Tight zigzag stitches also form buttonholes and appliqué borders.

ACKNOWLEDGMENTS

Thanks to Sameena Ahmad, Marc Swanson, Jenny Gossmann, Jason & Erin Mullin,
Agnieszka Gasparska, Beci Orpin & family, Caroline Greeven and Marc Gerald from The Agency Group,
Bulfinch Press, Deborah Kreilling and Judy Raymond from Simplicity Patterns, Rhiannon Kubicka,
Eviana Hartman, Goodesign, Michael Calderone, John Dominguez, and Wallace Fludd.

INDEX

© MELODIE MCDANIEL

Wendy Mullin has been sewing for more than twenty years. She is the designer of the Built by Wendy clothing line, founded in 1991. Originally from suburban Chicago, she currently lives and works in New York City. For more about Wendy, you may visit her Web site www.builtbywendy.com. For more on Wendy's patterns, you may visit www.Simplicity.com.

Eviana Hartman is an editor at *NYLON* magazine, and was formerly a fashion writer at both *Vogue* and *Teen Vogue.* She was a novice sewer when she first met Wendy but has since made, among other things, an elaborate braided-strap dress and monogrammed puffy bedroom slippers for her family. She lives in Brooklyn, New York.

Beci Orpin lives in Melbourne, Australia, with her son, Tyke; partner, Ralph; and cat, Miso. She graduated RMIT with a BA in textile design in 1997. In addition to her own clothing line, Princess Tina, she has designed graphics, textiles, and illustrations for Burton Snowboards, HarperCollins, Levi's, Etnies Shoes and Dark Horse Comics. She has been working with Built by Wendy for the past five years. For more about Beci, you may visit her Web site www.beciorpin.com.

Additional illustrations by **Agnieszka Gasparska.** You may visit her Web site www.kissmeimpolish.com.